T0062025

On John Stuart Mill

CORE KNOWLEDGE

CORE KNOWLEDGE

The Core Knowledge series takes its motivation from the goals, ideals, challenges, and pleasures of Columbia College's Core Curriculum. The aim is to capture the intellectual energy and the stimulus to creative thinking that is a fundamental ideal of such courses as Literature Humanities and Contemporary Civilization. In the spirit of Core teaching, the books are intended to reflect on what the featured works *can* be if approached from different or unusual vantage points; how they may inform modern experience, and how they are to be viewed not as sources of plain fact, certainty, and assured beliefs but as provocations to the imagination that help us to see differently, experimentally, and with a spirit of intellectual adventure.

On
John Stuart Mill

Philip Kitcher

Columbia University Press / New York

Columbia University Press
Publishers Since 1893
New York   Chichester, West Sussex
cup.columbia.edu
Copyright © 2023 Columbia University Press

Library of Congress Cataloging-in-Publication Data
Names: Kitcher, Philip, 1947– author.
Title: On John Stuart Mill / Philip Kitcher.
Description: New York : Columbia University Press, 2023. |
    Series: Core knowledge | Includes bibliographical references
    and index.
Identifiers: LCCN 2022027704 (print) | LCCN 2022027705 (ebook) |
    ISBN 9780231204149 (hardcover) | ISBN 9780231204156
    (trade paperback) | ISBN 9780231555395 (ebook)
Subjects: LCSH: Mill, John Stuart, 1806–1873.
Classification: LCC B1607 .K58 2023 (print) | LCC B1607 (ebook) |
    DDC 192—dc23/eng/20220817
LC record available at https://lccn.loc.gov/2022027704
LC ebook record available at https://lccn.loc.gov/2022027705

Columbia University Press books are printed
on permanent and durable acid-free paper.

Printed in the United States of America

Cover design: Lisa Hamm
Cover image: Alamy

To the students in my sections of Contemporary Civilization and to the graduate student preceptors with whom I have worked, with thanks for many hours of fruitful and instructive conversation.

And in memory of Deborah Martinsen, whose warmth and commitment to students have done so much for general education at Columbia.

Contents

Preface

When sessions of Columbia's extraordinary Core Course, Introduction to Contemporary Western Civilization (more usually known as "Contemporary Civilization" or just "CC") come fully alive for a group of twenty-two sophomores—and that is by no means a rare event—everyone in the room, students and teacher alike, is no longer simply absorbing the ideas of some thinker from the past but actively relating the author's words to the circumstances of the day. CC is not merely concerned with digesting the chunks of wisdom supplied by the Great Dead, according to some recipe supplied by conventional scholarship. At its best, it consists in an interrogation of the text from which first-time readers and seasoned experts may learn.

The excitement of finding new treasures in familiar places is one of the great joys of teaching this course, especially savored by those who have the privilege of serving a three-year term working with the graduate student preceptors who are teaching it for the first time. I have enjoyed that privilege. As one of my predecessors told me in advance, it is a "dream job." His assessment is entirely accurate.

The short book that follows is written in the spirit of CC. Often, as I was writing it, snatches of conversations from sections I had taught and from the preceptors' seminar percolated through my thoughts. In some ways, John Stuart Mill is one of the easiest of the canonical authors on the syllabus. He is surely a towering figure in the history of liberalism, and he articulates some of its central themes with unsurpassed clarity. Yet he also inspires a sense of banality: his thoughts may once have been startling, but they are so no longer. Since everything he had to tell us has been absorbed, why do we need to go back to read his seminal essays?

For a simple reason. We are overconfident, believing that we have fully understood him. I hope some of the subsequent pages will shake that confidence.

I am extremely grateful to Elisabeth Ladenson and Gareth Williams for inviting me to submit a proposal for a volume on Mill in the series they edit. Both of them assisted me in preparing that proposal and gave me constructive suggestions on a previous draft of the whole book. Several readers for Columbia University Press have offered excellent advice (most of which I have taken) on the proposal and on the full text. I have also benefited enormously from the reactions of my old UCSD comrades Richard Arneson and David Brink, as well as from detailed discussions with my Columbia friend and colleague, the distinguished legal scholar Vincent Blasi, a fellow aficionado of Milton—and of Mill.

Sadly, the principal architect of this book series, Deborah Martinsen, did not live to see the publication of any of the volumes. In 2020, after decades of contributing to Columbia as a distinguished scholar of Dostoyevsky, as a teacher of Russian language and literature, and, perhaps most prominently, as a brilliant administrator of the Columbia Core, Deborah was diagnosed with pancreatic cancer. All those of us who worked with her vividly recall the breadth of her learning, the thoroughness she devoted to make Core courses run smoothly, and the kindness and good cheer with which she warmed students and faculty alike. Columbia will miss her.

On John Stuart Mill

1

The Making of a Conflicted Humanist

e peers out at us earnestly, somewhat quizzically, as if he had important things to tell us and was slightly unsure of our abilities to comprehend them. The high forehead advertises a life devoted to thinking, and, indeed, those partial to the dubious enterprise of retrospective attributions of "general intelligence" typically award him "one of the highest IQs of all time." The sprouting tufts of hair and the uneven whiskers suggest a lack of personal vanity. John Stuart Mill appears to have his powerful mind trained on the important things.

What is the message he is concerned to deliver? And to whom is it addressed?

Let's begin with the second question. Mill is typically classified as a philosopher (and, on the side, as a contributor to economics), and his interpreters write books about his impact on the Western philosophical tradition. Some of those books are excellent, making strong cases for his continued importance for contemporary professional philosophy. Yet unlike most of the writers from the past two centuries whom we label as "philosophers," Mill never held an academic post. His impressive stream of books and articles issued from a working life spent as an official of the East India Company and, later on, as a member of Parliament. University professors read what he wrote. So too did most leading figures in British society, their counterparts in other countries, as well as a vast number of other people, from young students to established scholars in all sorts of fields. His readers and interlocutors included French socialists like Charles Fourier and Louis Blanc; the Italian revolutionary Giuseppe Mazzini; the French positivist Auguste Comte; the British novelist George Eliot and her paramour, the polymath G. H. Lewes; and the British prime minister William Gladstone (who referred to Mill, after his death, as "the saint of rationality.") Undergraduates at St. Andrews University elected him as their rector. Large numbers of politicians, novelists, economists, and scientists paid serious attention to what he had to say. Like many other philosophers in the past (but not in the present), John Stuart Mill wrote for that possibly imaginary entity, the generally educated public.

That fact inclines me to approach him differently. Instead of seeking what he has to tell contemporary philosophers interested in ethics or political philosophy or epistemology, I want to excavate what—if anything—he offers to the contemporary descendants of his Victorian audience. What relevance does he have to the concerns of politicians, economists, scientists, and literary figures in the early twenty-first century? Why should young people, engaged in an already overloaded course of studies, read Mill today? Why do some of his writings belong on the syllabi of ambitious courses in general education? Why, for example, is he required reading for Columbia University's great "Core Course," Introduction to Contemporary Western Civilization?

Perhaps these questions should be answered by rejecting their presupposition. While Mill retains his significance for professional philosophy, while he may once have addressed a broad public, his writings no longer have any general interest. He should be dropped from the syllabi. His world is too far from our own. The wider public has already absorbed everything he has to teach. Contemporary readers will become painfully aware of the limitations of his discussions, even where, as with respect to female emancipation, he was most resolute in championing a cause. Looking back, we may sympathize with the assessment offered by one of his contemporaries—Karl Marx, impoverished, seated in the unheated reading room of the British Museum, resentful of the contrast between his own obscurity and Mill's fame, saw his rival as a minor elevation (a pimple) on a flat plain. Or we might endorse Monty Python's judgment of Mill's offerings as a weak brew: "John Stuart Mill, of his own free will, on half a pint of shandy was particularly ill."

I hope to show that skeptical dismissals are wrong. As in his own century, many people should find it worthwhile to read Mill today.

────

Mill's smooth and accessible style deceives the modern reader. The Victorian elegance, the polish of his prose, the apparent lucidity, combine to convey an impression of calm and order. The message is diluted because there seems to be no need to probe. We easily miss the turmoil underneath. Slotting him into familiar categories, we praise him for ideas we take ourselves to understand completely. With condescending gratitude, we recognize insights we owe to him, ideas and ideals whose limitations we take him to overlook. His most famous works, *Utilitarianism* and *On Liberty*, metamorphose: they become *Mill for Dummies*.

"Everyone knows" that Mill was a utilitarian. He followed Jeremy Bentham in holding that to act rightly is to maximize happiness. You maximize happiness if, as a result of what you do, the largest available excess of pleasure over pain is created. To be sure, Mill adds a novel twist to Bentham's account. Bentham, he claims, failed to recognize important distinctions among pleasures. Some, like the crude games played in the pub, are "lower"; others, reading poetry for example, are "higher." The proper measurement of happiness must adjust accordingly—a lesser amount of some higher pleasure may outweigh a greater amount of a lower pleasure (although Mill doesn't explain exactly how the accounting is to be done).

"Everyone also knows" that Mill was an ardent defender of individual liberty. Freedom, he tells us, consists in choosing and pursuing your own good in your own way. Intervention in the lives of others is warranted only to prevent their harmful impingement on how other folk live. Important points indeed—but well absorbed in contemporary social and political life. Sometimes, of course, they are stretched too far and misinterpreted, transformed into a fanatical libertarianism. Perhaps Mill himself was tempted to go a long way in this direction.

A two-paragraph précis of *Mill for Dummies*. It provokes an obvious question: How do these two sets of ideas hang together? Fortunately, Mill tells us. His defense of liberty, he explains, makes no reference to rights that are independent of utility. The argument of *On Liberty* is thoroughly utilitarian. He writes: "I regard utility as the ultimate appeal on all ethical questions; but it must be utility in the largest sense, grounded on the permanent interests of man as a progressive being." But now we have to ask: What is Mill's conception of the good? Is it presented in *Utilitarianism*, in terms of happiness? Or is it the "largest sense" characterized in *On Liberty*? Could it be *both*? If not, which work has priority?

Superficially, of course, "the permanent interests of man as a progressive being" sounds rather different from "the excess of pleasure over pain." But let's not worry too much. After all, Mill has adjusted Bentham's version of utilitarianism to accommodate the higher pleasures. Let's think of these higher pleasures as becoming available to our species as history unfolds progressively. *On Liberty* can then be read as based on the ethical view presented in *Utilitarianism*, a view it characterizes in an exalted, rather flowery way. Problem solved. No tension between the two essays. Mill is the smooth, consistent—and shallow?—thinker we always took him to be.

Let's pause here. Is it right to treat the two formulations as equivalent and to wave vaguely in the direction of style? Does *Mill for Dummies* overlook a real and interesting tension, one that introduces complexities in his thought? Instead of trying to impose what we think of as the view from *Utilitarianism* on a different text, it's worth asking if we really understand Mill's departure from Bentham. A different strategy would be to consider, independently, what he might have meant by "grounded on the permanent interests of man as a progressive being." Pursuing that strategy might lead us to understand his ethics differently. It might also expose him as recognizing problems and inconsistencies that trouble reflective people today. And we might learn from Mill's attempts to wrestle with these problems.

As will become clear, this strategy yields a different Mill from the smooth—and irrelevant?—character who figures in *Mill for Dummies*. He's more conflicted and more interesting. But that's not the only reason for taking him seriously. He's there, openly addressing us, in other writings. Though I don't want to claim that the progressive Mill (as I'll call him) is the One True Genuine Article, he has at least as much right to that title as the protagonist of *Dummies*. And he does have a message for our times.

⸙

When you start to look hard, a celebration of human progress is all over Mill's corpus. At the end of a book largely devoted to methodology, the *System of Logic*, he closes a discussion of the social sciences with an extraordinary, almost poetic passage where he contrasts two senses of happiness. On the one hand, the "comparatively humble" sense refers to "pleasure and freedom from pain"; on the other, the "higher meaning" takes happiness to reside in living a "life, not what it now is almost universally, puerile and insignificant, but such as human beings with highly developed faculties can care to have." This contrast runs through many other works, in which what is fundamentally valuable is understood in terms of a kind of human progress— and, as many of Mill's detractors would emphasize, it sometimes leads him to make offensive claims about the backwardness of nations and of social groups whose cultural achievements he fails to appreciate. The theme recurs at the close of the long address given at St. Andrews when he took up his post as rector. After almost three hours of a disquisition on the purposes of higher education, Mill concludes with a resounding endorsement of the arts for their enrichment of human lives, through which an individual is able "to leave his fellow creatures some little better for the use he has known how to make of his intellect."

Passages like these signal the presence of subterranean waters that bubble up through the surface of Mill's prose, often in what seem the most improbable places. The deep flow of his thought is driven by a concern to *realize* the "permanent interests of" humanity. To allow human lives to go better. To transform societies so they become healthier.

The progressive Mill doesn't ground his thinking in utilitarian ethics or in a celebration of human freedom. His most fundamental commitment is to a distinctive type of humanism. Our species, as he conceives it, is engaged in a transgenerational project, one in which individual human beings make their own distinctive contributions to a far larger enterprise. Not to creating the kingdom of God on Earth but to helping, in small but cumulative ways, successive generations advance beyond the "puerile and insignificant" lives that have, historically, been the lot of most people, to forms of life that "human beings with highly developed faculties can care to have." His extended review of education and its aims culminates in explaining to the St. Andrews undergraduates the point of their studies: they are to "leave [their] fellow creatures a little better."

Given Mill's own education, his espousal of this form of humanism shouldn't come as a shock. He imbibed Greek thought, if not with his mother's milk, at least with his father's monstrous discipline. The works he read (in the original) during his early years revolved around a question—posed most pithily by Socrates—to which ancient authors revert again and again: How to live? In fact, as Mill saw, more clearly than previous thinkers, the question takes two connected forms: "How should *I* live?" and "How should *we* live together?" Neither can be addressed independently of the other. To probe the character of a flourishing life for an individual, one must understand how that individual relates to others; to identify the characteristics of a healthy society, it is necessary to recognize how societies promote or detract from the lives of their members.

Mill's humanism is the principal renewal of Greek thought in the Anglophone tradition, a secular, liberal response to the Socratic question(s). As we shall see, his liberalism constitutes an important departure from the ancient approaches to the issues. Yet before we embark on exploring the details, it's important to avoid another temptation to simplify. Surface qualities again entice readers to go astray. It's easy to read the references to "highly developed faculties" too narrowly. Or, inspired by the well-known portraits, to conceive human progress in terms of intellectual advances. The high forehead and apparent disdain for appearance prompt a vision of the progressive Mill as emphasizing cold, cognitive growth. Human beings become better able to think, acquiring new skills for "deliberation." Our species transcends the puerile condition by overcoming the brutish passions, subordinating them to a hyperdeveloped intellect.

The image of the dispassionate reformer is an improvement on *Mill for Dummies*, but my version of the progressive Mill is more full-blooded. He's not someone who might sip, demurely, at half a pint of shandy. Throughout his life, Mill was strongly moved, dedicated to championing causes, some of them apparently hopeless (like female suffrage). The human project he envisages is not simply assessed by noting steps toward high-mindedness. It is also a progress of sentiments.

To avoid diagnosing him as an anemic progressive, the best medicine is to review the details of Mill's life.

⸺⸺

John Stuart Mill was born in 1806 in London. His father, James Mill, was a wide-ranging intellectual, moving in radical circles and writing on philosophical, social, and political topics. During his son's early years, the elder Mill was much occupied with his magnum opus, *The History of British India*, a highly critical study of the administration of the subcontinent by the East India Company. After its publication in 1817, James Mill was employed by the company and charged with reforming it. His son would eventually succeed him in this role.

Famously, the father devised an extraordinary educational regime for his firstborn. John Stuart began Greek at three, moving on to Latin and Hebrew before he had reached his teens. The boy's precocity may have inspired James to turn the educational screw ever more rigorously. Much influenced by his friends Jeremy Bentham and David Ricardo (the most eminent economist of the age), the elder Mill groomed his son to become the leading advocate of utilitarian philosophy and socioeconomic reform for the next generation. In his early teens, having read extensively in English history, as well as digesting far more Greek and Latin texts than contemporary undergraduates majoring in classics typically study, John Stuart started a paternal "course" in political economy, primarily based on the writings of Ricardo. The teenager's first emergence into public intellectual life came with his publication of articles taking up "unsolved problems" in Ricardo's work, originally assigned by his father as homework exercises.

Despite the younger Mill's apparent successes and his energetic participation in discussions with men who either were already or would become intellectual leaders in British society, the rigors of his education eventually took their toll. In 1826, he fell into a deep depression, one he later took to be most aptly described by Coleridge in the "Ode on Dejection." As he explains in his *Autobiography*, since 1821 and his reading of Bentham, he had a clear conception of his identity: "I had what might truly be called an object in life: to be a reformer of the world." During the period when the "cloud" descended upon him, he posed a direct question to himself: " 'Suppose that all your objects in life were realized; that all the changes in institutions and opinions which you are looking forward to could be completely effected at this very instant: would this be a great joy and happiness to you?' And an irrepressible self-consciousness immediately answered, 'No!' At this my heart sank within me: the whole foundation within which my life was constructed fell down." Crushed by his dejection, Mill asked himself how long he might be able to bear his gloom. Not more than a year, he thought.

The first small illumination was prompted by reading a memoir, in which the author recalls how, when a young boy whose father had recently died, he consoled himself by a "sudden inspiration": that "he would be everything to [his family]—would supply the place of all they had lost." Mill testifies to his own "vivid conception of the scene and its feelings," and, from the resulting tears, "his burthen grew lighter." References to emotion in his retrospective understanding of how he began to recover are not accidental. For as he relates the subsequent process of healing, a crucial step comes with a new appreciation of the significance of the "internal culture of the individual": "I ceased to attach almost exclusive importance to the ordering of outward circumstances, and the training of the human mind for speculation and action. I had now learnt by experience that the passive susceptibilities needed to be cultivated as well as the active capacities, and required to be nourished and enriched as well as guided."

The education of Mill's sentiments was carried forward by two major tutors. He had heard, he tells us, that art and poetry are "important instruments of human culture." Yet of all the arts, only music had spoken directly to him, and, in his period of despair, he found himself deaf to its charms. Poetry seemed no better able to bring relief—he "got no good" from a thorough reading of Byron. Wordsworth, however, proved to be a different matter, and not simply because of his "beautiful pictures of natural scenery":

What made Wordsworth's poems a medicine for my state of mind, was that they expressed, not mere outward beauty, but states of feeling, and of thoughts coloured by feeling, under the excitement of beauty. They seemed to be the very culture of the feelings, which I was in quest of. In them I seemed to draw from a source of inward joy, of sympathetic and imaginative pleasure, which could be shared in by all human beings; which had no connexion with struggle or imperfection, but would be made richer by every improvement in the physical or social condition of mankind.

In discovering the importance of a new aspect of human life and culture, one from which he had previously been excluded, Mill reformulated his identity as a progressive reformer. He did not abandon his goal of making the world better, improving the conditions of human life, and promoting human flourishing. Instead, he learned that emotions recollected in tranquility added new dimensions to his life and to the lives of others. There was no "turning away from, but . . . a greatly increased interest in, the common feelings and common destiny of human beings."

Wordsworth brought him out of his "habitual depression." The full work of transformation was not yet complete, however. In 1830, Mill met the woman who was to become the love of his life. Unfortunately, Harriet Taylor was already married to John Taylor, a London druggist. Two years younger than Mill, "she was a beauty and a wit," and he rhapsodizes on her "gifts of feeling and imagination" and her "fiery and tender soul." Mr. Taylor apparently lacked "the intellectual or artistic tastes which would have made him a companion for her." Out of respect for a man whom he describes as "upright, brave, and honourable," Mill and Taylor supposedly did not consummate their mutual attraction, although they were excluded from some social circles in which their relationship was regarded as scandalous. In 1851, however, two years after Mr. Taylor had obligingly died, the pair finally married.

Does the long interval signal the refined, "Platonic" character of the relationship? Was this a cerebral match, merely "a marriage of true minds"? Certainly, Mill and Taylor admired each other's intellects. She seems to have found in him the intellectual companion she had always yearned for. He compares her—favorably!—to Shelley and consistently portrays her as a coauthor, equally responsible for the development of the ideas that appear under his name. Should we imagine them, prim and restrained, taking tea in a Victorian parlor, happily sharing lofty thoughts?

Not at all. First, Mill recognizes his relationship with Taylor as a continuation, a further fulfillment, of the healing process begun by Wordsworth. He had begun to learn how to feel, and this rapidly developing friendship brought a new sense of the depth and significance of the sentiments. Second, his evident desire for her company alarmed some of his friends. Mill rejected their urgings to be more discreet, more socially prudent, and, in some instances, their cautions weakened or even ruptured the friendship. Third, and most crucial, is the evidence of the surviving correspondence. In late July 1832, in response to a letter from Taylor telling him that they must not meet again, Mill replies (in French). He blesses the hand that has written to him—although its message is to "tell [him] an eternal farewell," a farewell she knows he can never accept. Although their paths are to be separate, "they can, they must, rejoin." He will obey her—he will not add "one drop" more to her "cup of sufferings." Of course, the supposed parting does not occur. A year or so later, she is addressing him as "my love" and assuring him that she is "loved as I desire to be." Neither of them is as explicit as a typical twentieth- or twenty-first-century writer (especially, perhaps, on social media), but, one morning in 1833, Taylor writes Mill a letter, ostensibly to reassure him: "Far from being unhappy or even low this morning, I feel as tho' you had never loved me half so well as last night." Whatever occurred on the evening (or night) before, her words surely signal events she had feared in 1832, demonstrations of ardent affection that had provoked her request for an "eternal farewell." Knowing that Mill will wonder if they have gone too far, she writes—early—to tell him that she now accepts, is even happy, with his attentions. A letter from September 1833 makes this fully explicit: "I am glad that you have said it—I am *happy* that you have—no one with any fitness & beauty of character but must feel compelled to say *all*, to the being they really love, or rather with any *permanent* reservation it is not *love*." She concludes, after three or four further pages: "*Dearest* I have only five minutes in w^h to write this or I should say more—but I was obliged to say something before tomorrow. t'was too long to wait dearest."

The warmth and the ardor are reciprocal. Deprived of the opportunity to be in each other's constant presence, they are forced to write apologies for potential misunderstandings. A letter from Mill begins: "I have been made most uncomfortable all day by your dear letter sweet & loving as it was dearest one—because of your having had that pain—& because of my having given you pain." Hypersensitive to her feelings, Mill chides himself for having failed to understand something she had wanted to say and urges her to convey everything that is important to her: "Why did you not make me feel that you were saying what was important to you, & what had not been said or exhausted before? I am writing to you in complete ignorance about what it was." Like Taylor, he cannot wait until their next meeting: "I know darling it is very doubtful you will get this before I see you—but I cannot help writing it." He concludes by addressing her "mine own—o you dear one." To which Taylor adds four words (written, presumably, after she had read it): "my *own adored* one."

In the 1830s, people who were not romantically involved did not usually use this kind of language.

Harriet Taylor died in 1858 in Avignon. After her death, accompanied by his stepdaughter, Helen, Mill spent an increasingly large part of the year in the house he and Harriet had purchased in Avignon so that he and Helen could pay daily visits to the grave. The lessons Harriet and Wordsworth had taught him had been fully absorbed.

───※※※───

Those lessons left an early and enduring imprint on his writings. During the 1830s, Mill published articles that would strike orthodox Benthamites as a waste of time—or worse. He offered a passionate plea for funding of the arts and voiced his appreciation for poets, some established, others emerging. In 1838 and 1840, twin essays appeared, the first on Bentham, the second on Coleridge. To my mind, these essays have not been given their due. Together, they expose the sources of conflict in Mill's progressive humanism—and they should direct us toward exploring his attempts to resolve the tensions.

Any attempt to treat Mill's approach to ethical, social, and political issues by regarding him as tinkering with the Benthamite framework of his early education should come to terms with his clear-eyed assessment of Bentham's achievements and deficiencies. By 1838, both James Mill and Jeremy Bentham were dead, and Mill's appreciation could be coupled to an unsparing diagnosis of Bentham's limitations. Sympathetic to Bentham's reformist impulses—particularly to his desire to "let each count for one, and none for more than one," an inclusive commitment to considering the welfare of all human beings, indeed of all sentient animals, in settling moral and social questions—Mill is unusually harsh in judging Bentham's conception of what human well-being consists in. "Man, that most complex being, is a very simple one in Bentham's eyes." Mill diagnoses the failure in language that surely echoes his own history, the early force-feeding, the breakdown, and the route he had traced in his recovery: Bentham fails to comprehend "the more complex forms of the feeling [sympathy]—the love of loving, the need for a sympathizing support or for objects of admiration and reverence." In short, "He saw . . . in man little but what the vulgarest eye can see." Hardly the tribute of a devoted disciple, this verdict leads Mill to a startling conclusion: "There is no need to expatiate on the deficiencies" of Bentham's system of ethics.

Bentham's incomprehension of the varieties and depths of the emotions is reflected in his dismissive attitude to the arts and to poetry. The companion essay turns to a poet, celebrating Coleridge's understanding of aspects of the human condition that Bentham and his disciples miss. In Mill's view, that leads them to cheapen their reforms by concentrating on only part of what human beings and societies need. Coleridge, the conduit for Kantian philosophy into the Anglophone world, as well as a reviver of long-standing traditions, would be (on both grounds) anathema to the self-styled progressives among whom Mill grew up. Yet, he claims, Coleridge himself is a kind of progressive, someone who intends to *revive* important parts of human life currently in decay and decline. Bentham and Coleridge should be viewed as complementary, the one rightly recognizing the need for an inclusive set of reforms, the other insisting that those reforms attend to all aspects of the human condition and not merely to those that can be easily and superficially noted (by those with the "vulgarest eyes"). Mill sees Coleridge as recognizing the need to *develop* individuals, cultivating their "higher" sentiments (which cannot be expected to arise spontaneously), and for them to absorb a sense of community ("cohesion") with one another.

Bentham and Coleridge each emerge as one-sided, each emphasizing an important truth, each blind to the insight achieved by the other. Both instantiate a condition Mill emphasizes in *On Liberty*'s famous defense of the freedom of discussion: limiting public debate entrenches opinions that have arrived at *part* of the truth and thus prevents them from being enlarged by an important complementary insight. Mill's progressivist program is to be founded on an envisaged synthesis. He still identifies himself as "a reformer of the world," but one who has replaced Bentham's narrow vision of the human good with a more refined account of human character. In elaborating and applying that account, it will be important to recognize the role of the feelings simpleminded utilitarians neglect, to nurture poetic and artistic sensibilities, to acknowledge the significance of "the love of loving," to make room for objects of admiration and reverence, and to appreciate interpersonal ties and the bonds that exist within communities.

The progressivist project to which Mill dedicates himself is one built on this (potential) synthesis. Before reformers can intelligently design societies to foster the human good, they will have to arrive at an account of the human good—one that is more exact than gesturing at a list of valuable components. Mill's humanism faces the challenge of forging the synthesis, perhaps not completely, but with sufficient precision to point the way to progress.

It is a *hard* challenge, since many of the elements to which these essays (and their successors) point are not easy to reconcile.

Because of that fact, Mill is a *conflicted* humanist. Many of the tensions that tug him this way and that arise for individuals and for societies today. Perhaps we can learn from his struggles.

⸺⸎⸺

The chapters that follow focus on four areas in which Mill's thought is torn. *On Liberty* emphasizes a fundamental freedom, grounded in the ability to choose the pattern of your own life and to pursue it as you think best. Everyone should have this freedom. Yet it is plainly possible for there to be friction, for my chosen project to interfere with yours. To preserve the integrity of the spaces in which people make their autonomous decisions, it's thus necessary to limit choice. My selection of goals and my decisions about how to pursue them cannot be allowed to restrict your kindred selections and decisions. Mill advocates a "Harm Principle": I am free to choose so long as my choices do not harm others; my liberty to swing my fist stops before your jaw (*just before?*). A vast amount of excellent learned commentary has attempted to articulate this principle—and, indeed, Mill begins the work himself. When, however, the idea of freedom for all is embedded in the richer conception of human life Mill envisages as he reflects on Bentham's limitations, the scope for potential interference is radically expanded, for two reasons. First, given his commitment to the full development of individual capacities, emotional as well as cognitive, understanding the limits on free choice must take into account the many ways that human growth can be stunted. Second, given the importance Mill places on relationships, particularly his appreciation of the possibilities of love, the connections among people allow for the transmission of injury. Your life suffers from the hindrances that beset those to whose welfare you are dedicated. Harm can no longer be confined, either to the obvious forms of material deprivation or to the life of a single, isolated individual. As we shall see, many of the most difficult social dilemmas affecting contemporary societies stem from our tacit—and partial—recognition of the conflicts exposed when a rich humanism, like Mill's, is taken seriously.

That humanism also complicates his most conspicuous contribution. Chapter 2 of *On Liberty* is often read and discussed in isolation from the rest of the text, hailed as a classic defense of free speech. Yet it is set in the context of a discussion of individual freedom based on his high standards of human development and is followed by a celebration of individuality. As Mill clearly recognizes, the actual practices of free and open exchange of ideas can easily undermine the principal claim of democracy: to wit, that it empowers the citizens and enhances their freedom. In a world where misinformation leads many voters to choose leaders whose policies are at odds with the goals they cherish most, Mill's attempts to understand how democracy can promote freedom continue to be relevant. Here too different aspects of his humanism need to be reconciled. One impulse pulls him to celebrate free speech; another expresses his recognition that the superficial machinery of democracy—elections preceded by open discussion—is worthless unless it accords with special conditions, including requirements on what can be said (and how it can be said). If this tension is to be relieved, it will be, I suggest, through elaborating the notion of social cohesion—of fellow citizenship—Mill appreciates in Coleridge.

Debates about equality (and inequality) constitute a third domain in which Mill's conflicts are ours. The passionate emphasis on autonomy and on individuality found in chapters 1 and 3 of *On Liberty* is in tension with his deep commitment to the development of *all*. Mill is no Nietzsche, interested only in the full flourishing of the few, the "free spirits," and prepared to let "the herd" go hang. He retains, to the end, his Benthamite conviction that "each is to count for one and none for more than one." His posthumous *Chapters on Socialism*, lovingly edited by his adopted daughter, Helen, reveals how hard he struggled to determine the limits of political, social, and economic inequality. A third chapter of *Mill for Dummies* might portray him as an unabashed libertarian, a passionate advocate of capitalism with unregulated ("free"?) markets. But whether he is doing economics or philosophy (or both together), progressive Mill is a far different character, constantly taxed in the attempt to make Bentham and Coleridge cohere.

Although almost all discussions of Mill, from *Dummies* to the most sophisticated, begin with his alleged utilitarianism, seeing it as the foundation for all his writings, the structure of Mill's ethics will be the final arena in which we survey his conflicted humanism. What exactly is Mill's conception of the good? How would he respond to contemporary ethical issues, questions today's thinkers sometimes address by wheeling out a version of utilitarianism (often one they take to descend from Mill)? I'll suggest relieving Mill of the title apparently merited by his authorship of a slim volume, frequently used to introduce readers to utilitarian ethics. He is, to be sure, a *consequentialist*, someone who holds actions to be right in virtue of the good they generate. But even if it proves impossible to resolve all the tensions in his rich conception of the good, there is, as we shall

see, an important gulf between his version(s?) of consequentialism and standard utilitarianism.

In his own day, Mill's humanist progressivism was most
apparent in a cause he took up early in his adult life: the emancipation of women. His commitment to it was reinforced by the
long relationship with Harriet and by his growing appreciation
of "what marriage may be in the case of two persons of cultivated faculties, identical in opinions and purposes, between
whom there exists that best kind of equality, similarity of powers and capacities with reciprocal superiority in them—so that
each can enjoy the luxury of looking up to the other, and can
have alternately the pleasure of leading and being led." When
he stood for Parliament, he made the (unpopular) promise to
introduce, if elected, a bill for female suffrage, and he kept his
promise (by introducing an amendment to Disraeli's Reform
Bill), garnering more votes in favor than would have been
expected. Yet I have chosen not to devote a chapter to Mill's
feminism, which appears most centrally in his classic essay *The
Subjection of Women*, a decision that may appear somewhat odd.
I have done so for a simple reason. My aim in this book is to
concentrate on themes in Mill that twenty-first-century thought
has not yet absorbed. People today should read Mill's passionate brief for expanding women's opportunities not for its *conclu-
sions* but for its brilliant analyses and argumentative strategies.
In Victorian England, Mill's version of feminism was exceptionally advanced, but while contemporary readers may warm to his
eloquent prose, they are likely (quite reasonably) to judge our
own age as transcending his views. Although they may applaud
his support of a flexible division of labor within the family,

another (politic?) concession may provoke raised eyebrows: Mill also contends, when domestic arrangements are "otherwise just," it is preferable to partition spheres of activity along traditional lines, for women to rear the children and not to work outside the home. No doubt the essay is an important text in the history of feminism—but for us its significance is different. It is a source of ideas that bear on many social and ethical issues, including those I discuss, yielding progressive insights we have not yet assimilated. Hence, in what follows, I shall often turn to it, although not for its "official" purposes.

Because Mill is a *conflicted* humanist, there are alternative ways to resolve the tensions in his position. My aim is to offer *one* coherent reading. Others might prefer to emphasize his commitment to meritocracy, at the cost of abandoning the theme he retained from his early education, that "each is to count for one and none for more than one." Bentham's dictum was the core of Mill's progressivism, and it endured throughout his life. Progressive Mill, as I shall present him, resolves the conflict between the claims of merit and the pull of equality by appeal to the principle that individuals count equally.

The man staring out from the picture does have messages for us. Progressive Mill, a thoroughly conflicted humanist, may not be able to solve all—or many, or any—of the large questions that trouble us most today. He is, however, in his tensions and struggles, a wonderful diagnostician. And he can supply us with tools that aid us in our own contemporary efforts.

2

Freedom for All?

In our time, as in Mill's, talk of freedom is omnipresent. Loudest, perhaps, in the vocal protests of those who believe their freedoms to have been restricted by the actions of evil oppressors. So, as I write, as a new surge of infectious disease threatens to overwhelm hospitals in parts of the United States, angry people carry placards complaining that mandates to wear masks in particular public spaces—in schools, for example—violate their liberties. In the recent past, similar levels of indignation have been inspired by anxieties about the possibility of prohibiting American citizens' access to weapons designed for efficient slaughter in theaters of war and by the laments of the wealthiest, piqued by the limits on their distribution of largesse to the war chests of their political protégés.

Any serious attempt to appraise the complaints and to resolve the debates to which they give rise must address some philosophical questions about freedom. What should count as freedom? Are some forms of freedom more important than others? How can we reconcile conflicts, when liberties seem to clash? Is it possible for any society or any political state to achieve freedom for all?

Mill's *On Liberty* is one of the deepest explorations of these questions that has ever been written.

— ∞ —

Answers are already outlined in the opening section of this seminal essay. Mill explains that he is focused on the most significant type of freedom: "The only freedom which deserves the name is that of pursuing our own good, in our own way, so long as we do not attempt to deprive others of theirs, or to impede their efforts to obtain it." This pregnant sentence announces a distinctive approach to the ancient question "How to live?" Instead of attempting to offer a list of qualities a well-lived life should have, Mill proposes that that is up to the liver. He makes the notion of autonomous choice (derived from the German thinker Wilhelm von Humboldt) central to the good life. People should decide what is most important for them. The life you live should be your own.

Surely, this is an attractive thought. Throughout human history, the overwhelming majority of people have had the patterns of their lives thrust upon them. They have been confined by caste and sex and class. Or by the rigid expectations of their families. Behind Mill's sentence stand a wealth of reflections on the identity his father designed, and tried to impose, on his eldest son.

Yet is any old choice good enough to make a life worthwhile? Imagine someone who decides, in his youth, that what he most wants to do is to retire to a secluded place, spending his days counting and recounting the number of blades of grass in a particular area. That's his own good, and he pursues it in his own way, kneeling for eight hours each day, recording the daily totals, and (to prevent anyone else from fathoming the secret) rising from his deathbed to destroy his findings. His project for his life has been his own, and he has completed it with unusual success. Has he discovered an unprecedented way to live well? No. His "life plan" seems pathological and his pursuit of it pathetic.

A particular kind of freedom, then, is important for living well. Nevertheless, it does not seem to be enough. What else might be required?

Answering that question will help us understand how to frame the difficult issues with which we began. It will point us to ways of differentiating kinds of freedoms and of comparing the liberties over which people clash. *On Liberty* provides some clues to how Mill would have explained the pathology of the fanatical grass counter, particularly in the third section's celebration of individuality. To bring his approach fully into the light, I suggest, we would do well to elaborate his (conflicted) humanism.

Recall his regretful verdict on the ways in which most human beings have lived: their lives have been "puerile and insignificant," not of a type "such as human beings with highly developed faculties can care to have." Their plans of life have rarely been chosen freely, of course, but that isn't the deficiency on which Mill fastens in his sad assessment. Whatever choices there have been haven't been made by people with "highly developed faculties." The shortcomings are not purely cognitive; that is, they are not only defects in the ability to deliberate intelligently. The moral Mill drew from his own history, expressed in his comparative studies of Bentham and Coleridge, was that both the intellect and the emotions require cultivation. Just before he suffered his breakdown, he would have counted himself as making a free, fully autonomous, affirmation in pledging himself to continue Bentham's reforms, as Bentham conceived them. Nor in his young manhood could he regard his *intellect* as being insufficiently developed. What had gone wrong, as he recognized from 1830 on, had been a stunting of his emotional growth.

If the twenty-year-old Mill, committing himself to a life centered on the work he then conceived for himself, doesn't count as autonomous, who does? As we connect the pregnant sentence from *On Liberty* with Mill's conception of the progressive human project, the attractive idea of "fundamental freedom" as choosing and following the pattern for our lives starts to waver and dissolve. Doesn't the society into which children are born inevitably fix the horizons within which later choices are made? Don't parents and the other members of the community they inhabit shape and color all subsequent decisions? Mill saw the point with exceptional clarity in his discussion of the ways that women's conceptions of their roles and goals are limited: the "nature of women is an eminently artificial thing" produced by a mixture of "forced repression" and "artificial forcing." Even if, like Harriet Taylor—or like Mill—people later repudiate some of the attitudes absorbed from their early socialization, aren't they ultimately bound by the resources those who guide their development have supplied, making use of those resources to determine the character of the rejection and of the position into which they then settle? Can the choice of a "life plan" ever be "our own"? If not, can it express "the only freedom which deserves the name"—or, indeed, any kind of freedom at all?

The concept of autonomy, central to Mill's account, thus emerges as far more intricate than it initially appears. Skeptical dismissals are, however, unwarranted. For there is a difference between the assignment of a person to a particular way of life, based on his caste or her sex or their class, and the Benthamite grooming John Stuart Mill endured. A contrast also between his socialization and a more sensitive shaping of a nascent person—one, perhaps, involving the kind of education envisaged in Mill's inaugural address at St. Andrews. The individuality enthusiastically commended in chapter 3 of *On Liberty* doesn't presuppose a self, fully formed at birth, with its distinctive features that an ideal education would elicit. Even less does it suppose the newborn infant can defy external influences and assert its own full-blown Individuality. What we choose at *any* stage of our lives is inevitably fashioned and limited by interactions between a growing self and the environment (particularly the social environment) in which it is embedded. Yet those interactions can be more or less coercive. Force, in various guises, can turn the developing person in an externally fixed direction. Or the process can be a conversation—either an ugly shouting match in which one party dominates or a responsive process of mutual listening.

Inspiring as Mill's pregnant sentence is, it will need some rewriting if its import is to become clear and precise. Freedom is inevitably a matter of respects and degrees. That should lead us to think of *increasing* freedom in the progressive human project Mill envisages. A central mode of human progress, perhaps the only mode "worthy of the name," consists in enhancing the autonomy of the choices people make in figuring out who they are and what they want and in pursuing the goals they set for themselves—making them *freer* than they otherwise would have been. Achieving that depends on a dialogue between society and the growing individual, one in which the directions of growth are in tune with the inclinations exhibited at the current stage.

The progressive Mill is bent on *improving* human lives by removing *some* of the factors constraining choices of "our own good" and our ability to pursue it. He will be attentive to how cognitive and emotional capacities are blocked, distorted, or undernourished. That must have occurred, he would tell us, in the socialization of the misguided grass counter. That person cannot have achieved mature human sensibilities, such as comprehending the significance of love (and thus loving to love) and appreciating the perspective offered at the end of Mill's inaugural address, the "duty to leave our fellow creatures some little better for the use" of his intellect. Despite my claim in framing the example—that the grass counter chose his plan of life freely—substantial degrees of unfreedom affect his decision. It issues from diminished capacities.

Any judgment of freedom must be relative to context. To regard a person, living at a particular historical stage, as possessing "the only freedom which deserves the name" is not to view that person as completely unconstrained. Rather, it views the choice of the person's "own good," of the "life plan" and the pursuit of it, as exhibiting as much freedom as could be expected at that particular moment in history: the dialogue between ambient society and the growing self is as sensitive as that epoch will allow; the cultivation of the cognitive and emotional faculties is as fruitful as that age could achieve. A position of this kind can distinguish between the choices made by the aristocrat and his wife or by the master and his slave, even though all parties are bound by the ignorance, prejudices, and conventions of their times. Reconstructed in this way, the thought of the well-lived life as one exhibiting an autonomously chosen, autonomously pursued, and successful life plan escapes the principal objections standardly leveled against Mill's liberal approach. More to the present point, it enables us to illuminate issues about the balance of different freedoms.

———∞∞∞———

The second half of Mill's pregnant sentence foreshadows the ways that *On Liberty* has made its best-known impact. The idea of noninterference in harmless activities through which people pursue their "own good" stands behind many important social reforms. In 1957, for example, in a decade when several prominent Britons had been prosecuted (and convicted) under laws banning homosexual acts, the Wolfenden Committee's report echoed Mill: "It is not, in our view, the function of the law to intervene in the private life of citizens, or to seek to enforce any particular pattern of behavior." Ten years later, Parliament repealed the prohibition of homosexual acts between "consenting adults in private."

Mill was not only concerned to prevent the legal system from reaching into individual lives to restrict conduct that caused no harm to others. He also hoped to check the "social tyranny" occurring when the "likings and dislikings" of a majority are expressed in ostracism and intolerance. His attempt to define the proper sphere of political power and legal constraint is presented with the explicit hope of modifying public opinion, so that amending the law serves as the prelude to greater tolerance and even to full acceptance. The strategy has proved its worth. The hope was justified. Half a century on, although the work of eradicating prejudice is unfinished, the number of people who would give vent, even in private, to the Earl of Dudley's famous rant, is greatly diminished. Few today would declare: "I cannot stand homosexuals. They are the most disgusting people in the world. . . . Prison is much too good for them; in fact, that is a place where many of them like to go—for obvious reasons."

The application of Mill's principle to this famous example appears straightforward. The homosexual couple next door causes no harm to anyone when their lovemaking goes on behind closed curtains (when the act is thoroughly private). Even here, however, a concern might creep in, one that will arise more blatantly in other instances. Perhaps one of their neighbors is a maiden lady, kindly and tolerant in many respects but devout and sensitive. As she passes by to do her shopping or to arrange the flowers for the Sunday service, she shudders as she wonders what is going on behind those curtains. Her disgust is less violent than Dudley's but no less real. She feels that the pattern of her own life is blotched, that the values she has chosen are scorned and derided. If she had the words, she might confess that she has been inhibited in pursuing her own good in her own way.

We think we know what to say about this woman. She is offended, but she is not harmed. The interference with her freedom is negligible in comparison with that inflicted on her neighbors, if they are banned from expressing their love in the ways they do. *To appreciate autonomy as a matter of respects and degrees is a crucial step toward evaluating disharmonies among people's life plans.* Faced with a clash, we are to ask: Does the interference occur with respect to a choice affecting some domain recognized as central by any human being with developed faculties? How severe is the constraint imposed? Mill's essay on Bentham marks out the personal expression of love as a central facet of human life. And, if the chosen form of love "dare not speak its name," that is surely as deep a form of interference as any. What can the troubled woman place on the scales to balance these weighty losses?

Perhaps she or her contemporary successors can say something in response. As we shall see, further complexities need to be explored. For the moment, however, Mill's humanism seems to supply the tools for working through a famous historical example. Let's now elaborate it to address some of the debates that arise today.

⸺⸺

When one person's (or one group's) approach to what matters in life is hard to reconcile with that espoused by another, a conflict can arise in one of two main ways. The more obvious occurs when activities of one, aimed at achieving chosen goals, weaken the support for the similar activities of the other or introduce obstacles making the ends pursued more difficult to attain. You want to hold practices for your rock band in your apartment; I hope to hold rehearsals for my madrigal quartet next door at the same time. In cases like these, the personal choices of the good have already been made—maybe we're both professional musicians, with differing tastes—and they're assumed to have been relatively autonomous, formed through processes we imagine to elicit our individuality. In my example of the homosexual lovers and the maiden lady, the clash affects different aspects of the lives; here, with the neighboring musicians, it centers on the same domain.

The second mode, emerging from the progressive Mill's account of "degreed autonomy," erupts when one person's (or group's) pursuit of a chosen good, apparently selected autonomously, distorts—or even wrecks—the *development* of another's faculties, thus ruining any opportunity for autonomous choice. Conflicts of this kind are all over human history, and they continue today. They are found in some important challenges to prevalent patterns of socialization. Whenever societies appeal to supposedly authoritative texts, often hailed as sacred, to impose a particular role on some of their members (people of a particular caste, or race, or sex), reinforcing it with an education tailored to the intended role, they interfere with individual development by narrowing the horizons within which choice can be made. Many women in "traditional religious" societies may not have suffered from policies preventing them from pursuing the goals they will actually set for themselves—the conditioning they receive may be in complete harmony with the support offered for them to realize their "properly feminine" ends. Again, Mill offers a scathing denunciation of the ignorance out of which men have constructed the socially binding conception of those ends, concluding that such specifications will be "wretchedly imperfect and superficial . . . until women themselves have told all they have to tell." That requires, as he argues, vastly expanded educational opportunities, enabling women to *set* those goals, to find out who they are and what they might want their lives to be. Moreover, even when those opportunities have been provided, it is important to remain sensitive to the underlying analysis. Today, we might wonder if, in some secular societies, women whose fully developed faculties might have inclined them to assume "traditional roles" have been coerced into "being liberated." Are we *ever* completely done with the work of enabling people, all men as well as all women, to tell "all they have to tell"?

Recognizing this second structure, the narrowing of developmental choices, when it occurs is especially important. For it frees debate from the difficulties of evaluating the centrality of a particular domain of choice or the severity of a constraint. We don't have to ask, for instance, whether freedom in loving is more or less critical than freedom in matters of religion. On the one hand lies the unhampered pursuit of a particular chosen goal. On the other, what is at stake is the possibility of full development and the consequent capacity for autonomous choice *across the board*. Whatever the problems of weighing alternatives that arise with respect to the first type of clash, the situation here seems far simpler. An obvious rule of thumb: diminished liberty in one specific part of one's life cannot rank in importance with the loss of any ability for free choice.

Progressive Mill adopts that rule of thumb. It gives substance to his conception of "the only freedom which deserves the name."

―∞∞∞―

When COVID-19 first began to sweep around the globe, many people in many parts of the planet foresaw its defeat as coming with the discovery of an effective vaccine. Building on a long sequence of progressive developments in many fields— immunology, virology, and molecular biology—ingenious researchers worked hard to develop, unexpectedly quickly, the vaccines that would deliver the hoped-for relief. In the interval, however, the world had changed—or perhaps come to show openly what it had always been. Affluent countries began to immunize their grateful citizens, only to discover, well before population-level safety had been attained, that there were pockets of resistance—particularly large in the United States. So, with considerable generosity, "vaccine objectors" have given the virus a second chance.

On what basis? People who have refused to receive the jab—and who often object to wearing the masks that might protect them and the members of their communities—have claimed to be exercising their fundamental freedom. They cannot be compelled by government mandate to cover their faces or bare their arms to the needle. Although their intractable opposition conflicts with the plans and projects of their neighbors, can they claim a right to "pursue their own good in their own way"?

Their strident protests against "government overreach" reveal gross insensitivity to the *distribution* of liberties. Although they might frame their complaints by pitting concern for freedom against the interests of public health, that is a slanted formulation of the conflict. Assertion of their own freedom "deprives others of theirs." However they might characterize the losses that submitting to the needle or covering their faces would bring to their pursuits of their own good (and it is far from obvious how serious any such sacrifices would be), for many of their vulnerable neighbors, the deprivations are evident and consequential. They will assume significant risks by engaging in the everyday activities required of any attempts to attain their chosen ends. They will gamble with their health in going to work, in shopping for food, in attending religious ceremonies or family gatherings, in a host of forms of recreation. And, of course, in sending their young children—not yet eligible for vaccination—to school or to preschool programs.

For almost all parents, children's thriving ranks high on the list of "their own good." Whatever the defects of contemporary education (and there are many), most parents justifiably believe that, without access to in-person schooling, their children's present lives would be diminished and their future opportunities narrowed. Apparently, then, the freedom to refuse masks and vaccines comes with a far heavier cost for the like freedoms of other people, a substantial and specifiable set of reductions in those people's ability to "pursue their own good in their own way."

That is not, however, the end of the matter. Besides the first mode of conflict (just outlined), we should recognize the second. By promoting the spread of the virus through their communities, thus increasing the chances of infecting unvaccinated children, the refuseniks not only foster sporadic absenteeism both of pupils and their teachers; they also threaten the ability of schools to remain open. Suffering from a disrupted education, the young are given a lesser opportunity to develop the cognitive and emotional capacities through whose exercise they will make their choices of their own good. Refusal to help in the struggle against the pandemic doesn't simply interfere with many patterns of behavior through which people, young and old, pursue what is most important to them. It also diminishes the autonomy of a whole generation. When that point becomes clear, the protest against requirements and mandates should be recognized for the hollow (and selfish) sham it is. Progressive Mill, the dedicated champion of liberty, would fully appreciate this.

Nor can gun fetishism and the Second Amendment worship often lurking behind it be defended. Perhaps your kindly, gun-toting neighbor will appeal to Mill's pregnant sentence. "Don't worry," he volunteers, "you can have a gun, too, just as powerful as mine; so I'm not depriving you of your freedom; the Second Amendment applies to both of us." Of course, that simple equivalence misreads Mill. The conflict in question here isn't a matter of one person's doing X restricting another's ability to do X (as it is with musicians who have only a thin wall between them). It arises from a clash between "pursuits of one's own good." That kind of disharmony can occur far more broadly: your pursuit is expressed in your doing X, my kindred pursuit would be expressed in doing Y; your doing X reduces my ability to do Y, and vice versa. Heading to the woods and blowing hapless deer into minute pieces ("an AK47 is awesome!") isn't among my high priorities. There are, however, many things I want that flooding the world with powerful guns renders impossible.

It matters to me, for example, that people—not just my family, my friends, and my acquaintances, but millions I don't know—can walk the streets in safety. That children are not terrorized and traumatized by seeing their peers killed and maimed in front of them. That their schools are not invaded and entire classes massacred, with the survivors emerging only after hours of fearful hiding. That their education isn't punctuated by enforced drills, impressing on them the grim reality of their environment. That they do not resist going to school because of anxieties about what will happen there or along the way. That they can spend time with their friends, in parks and other public places, without dreading the sudden whirr of bullets over their heads.

I suspect I'm not idiosyncratic in thinking of attaining these ends as desirable, conditions it is important to maintain (even to improve). If that's so, then a large group of people suffers a diminution of freedom in consequence of the ways that the United States currently permits the sale, storage, and use of guns. The projects of the kindly neighbor could probably go forward with some significant adjustment of the permissive statutes on the books. He could manage without blasting the deer to smithereens (maybe an old-fashioned rifle would do). He could cope with the minor inconvenience of storing it in a secure locker in a public depot (perhaps at the local range). Since he has nothing to hide, he would not be greatly disturbed by rigorous background checks. Perhaps the rules could be relaxed a bit for his cousin, living in a remote location and wanting a weapon to ward off possible intruders. A blanket ban on automatic weapons, coupled to stringent storage requirements and thorough scrutiny of potential owners, is compatible with the free pursuit of any morally permissible use of guns.

Moreover, rather than restricting freedom, that bundle of reforms would enhance it. The tiny losses experienced by gun users (forfeiting whatever joys accrue from rapid spraying of bullets, having to remember to take the key to the locker, and so forth) are more than compensated by the liberation of many people—especially poor people—whose daily lives are inflected with fear. Bullets often have a way (indeed, more than one) of terminating the search for the chosen good. Beyond the more obvious, tragic effects lies the systematic reduction of freedoms, including forms of Mill's second mode of conflict. When the full development of the faculties of many young people is inhibited, through the constant threat of gun violence, whether witnessed or directed at their growing bodies; through the prudent adjustments they are forced to make and the activities in which they cannot join; through the traumas and the fears and the consequent disruption of their education, the cost in freedom is enormous. To remove or only partly to alleviate the limitations that cramp and deform young lives would vastly outweigh the "freedoms" mildly checked in reforming gun use.

The Millian argument rests on an empirical assumption: reforms of the kind proposed would have the consequences I have supposed. In particular, such reforms would expand the opportunities for development of the children who are currently deprived. Available statistics reveal the United States as an outlier among developing nations with respect to gun deaths (although a considerable proportion of these are suicides). Australia's mandatory gun buyback program was followed by a decrease in gun-related homicides (although some analysts have questioned whether the governmental intervention caused the drop). These two fragments of evidence hardly settle the issue, but they surely encourage exploring it further. It would be premature to claim that reforming gun use in the suggested fashion would dramatically cut gun violence, let alone remedy the conditions currently detracting from children's development. Better to see the proposed reform, in Mill's terms, as a justifiable "experiment of living," one that promises to contribute to overall freedom—and one that should be adopted if the empirical presupposition is confirmed.

❦

Or consider the current rules for contributing cash to political candidates. Extremely wealthy Americans have campaigned, successfully, for rules allowing them to distribute their largesse in ever larger dollops to aspiring lawmakers whom they expect to favor their interests. The courts have been sympathetic, holding that their right to free speech must be protected. Yet these privileged people belong to a large population of other citizens, each of whom, we may assume, shares equally in the right to speak.

If there were world enough and time, allowing unlimited speech to anyone and everyone would be no crime. The world in which we live is, however, finite. There is a public microphone, constituted by a whole array of media outlets, through which, during an extended (but, mercifully, still finite) electoral season, candidates for office transmit their messages to audiences of potential voters. Time at the microphone is a commodity, variously priced to recognize the differential chances of reaching the ears of large numbers of citizens. The more money a candidate receives, the larger the number of possible transmissions and the greater their effectiveness in making themselves heard. None of this, of course, guarantees success for those who amass the largest war chests. Nevertheless, it's reasonable to think there will be some rough correlation. Otherwise, why would so many candidates be so assiduous in cultivating the wealthiest donors and tailoring their messages to suit the inclinations of the paymasters?

Individual citizens, singly or in combination with others, can contribute to office seekers who appear to speak on their behalf. If they are poor, their donations are likely to be paltry in comparison with the funds given—or should we say "invested"?—by the billionaires. All would be well, of course, if there were a pre-established harmony, a fine balance of corporate largesse reflecting perfectly the distribution of voices among different sections of the electorate. Anyone who believes in that kind of invisible hand is unlikely to fare well in the rough-and-tumble world of contemporary capitalism. It is all too clear that the interests of the ultrawealthy, on the one hand, and the poor, on the other, are typically (though not invariably) diametrically opposed.

The poor, too, have a right to speak. Their success in pursuing their own good—*and in securing for their children the possibility of developing the faculties upon which autonomous choice of the good depends*—will be affected, for good or ill, by the attitudes of those who are elected to public office. Their fundamental freedom, "the only freedom which deserves the name," is thus enhanced or diminished insofar as they are able to amplify or are prevented from facilitating the messages of the candidates they identify as speaking on their behalf. (I assume, for present purposes, that their power to pick out those candidates is not badly compromised. We'll return to this assumption in the following chapter.) To the extent that their favorites' messages are swamped by the transmissions of the well-heeled, their freedom is reduced. In the great arena of public debate, they become impotent.

The judges and justices who have relaxed limits on the bounty allowed to flow from the richest members of American society have surely read Mill. His stirring defense of freedom of speech is a subtext of many of their decisions. Yet what they add to the freedoms of the few, people already privileged and equipped with ample resources for "pursuing their own good in their own way," is heavily outweighed by what they subtract from the freedoms of the many, the large mass of citizens whose own abilities to advance their chosen ends are already tightly constrained. Indifferent to questions of distribution, these judges make a profound moral mistake. They should read *On Liberty* again. For they have misunderstood it. Badly.

The argument begun here has farther-reaching consequences. In the following two chapters we shall look at some of them.

⨫⨼⨻

First, though, it is time to raise a complaint and to address it. The treatment of the three examples turns on judgments about the relative importance of particular aspects of different human lives. The losses suffered by one party are claimed to be "outweighed by" or "trivial in comparison with" the gains of freedom enjoyed by another. Verdicts of this kind issue from a place outside the lives and the experiences assessed. They are *external*, delivered from some privileged perspective, occupied by some godlike figure (perhaps one depicted by Michelangelo?). But who can aspire to sit in that judgment seat? Can I? Can Mill? Can anyone?

No. The objection points to an important lacuna in my treatment of conflicts in freedom. It deserves to be taken seriously. Reflecting on it will lead us to a progressive elaboration of progressive Mill's approach to freedom.

Confession: while they are salient for contemporary U.S. citizens, the three examples I have chosen make my life easy. Readers of books like this one are likely to nod sympathetically, agreeing with my accounting of gains and losses. (Those who don't will surely have raised the complaint earlier—and probably stopped reading.) Antivaxxers, gun toters, and amply compensated executives, however, might want to take the dialogue further. Considering a more complex example will help us see how to bring the Seat of Eternal Judgment down to earth.

Recall one classic application of Mill's ideas, the Wolfenden Report and its legal legacy. Today, young people grow up in a different world, one in which many of them wonder how it could ever have seemed justified to imprison gay men, to abuse and taunt gays and lesbians, and even to attack and torture them. Seventy percent of Americans support same-sex marriages, and news sources routinely show pictures of beaming couples, delighted in being able to declare and solemnize their love.

Yet some people, counterparts of the sensitive and devout maiden lady, are at odds with this brave new world. They try to steer clear of it. From time to time, though, it impinges on their own affairs. Let's reflect on a familiar type of interaction in a simple, idealized, tale.

The scene: a small town in the United States. George and Ed have lived together for three years now and have decided that the time has come to make their relationship official. Both of them are practicing Christians, and their marriage ceremony will take place in the church they attend regularly. Like most of their neighbors—indeed, most of their fellow townspeople—their minister fully supports their relationship and is delighted to hear of their decision. So far, so good.

As they plan their reception, they choose a particular bakery—widely viewed, in their circle, as the best in town—to provide their wedding cake. They've heard, vaguely, that the owners of the bakery are Christians of a different denomination, one that holds "more traditional views" about marriage. Confident that there will be no problem, they go to the shop to discuss the design of the cake and the lettering to be inscribed on it.

The owners, Malcolm and Lucy Baker, are polite but firm. They explain their refusal to accept the order. They have nothing personal against George or Ed. But they cannot, in good conscience, become involved in the violation of a sacrament. To bake this cake would, they say, be a sin. Devout Christians as they are, they are committed to avoiding sin.

Viewed from the outside, the clash of freedoms here seems truly petty. If the Bakers are adamant, George and Ed can surely go elsewhere to find a perfectly acceptable cake. Maybe it would be slightly less delicious (but who ponders the gustatory quality of a wedding cake, anyway?). Or, having avowed their faith, the Bakers could allow the couple to purchase one of the cakes they sell (without asking questions); George and Ed could find someone to make the final decoration. Tiny concessions by either side would bring about a resolution.

These external judgments miss the point. For they fail to enter the individual perspectives of the parties and the high stakes they see behind the conflict. The Bakers view what they are asked to do as a sin. George and Ed, fully aware of homosexuals' long struggle to obtain recognition, tolerance, and acceptance, regard the refusal as another reminder that the campaign is not over, that their power to speak their love remains hedged and qualified. A judge looking on may be impatient with both parties, attempting to calculate the relative sizes of two minute diminutions of freedom. Perhaps the judge would issue a verdict. One of the minuscule losses is less than the other.

External resolution can seem easy. A (straight) religious believer dismisses the couple's hurt and their anger: "You can't expect everybody to like you or to approve what you do. Nobody can. The Bakers belong to a small minority. Go somewhere else for your cake. It's not worth the fuss." An atheist (or secular humanist) may denounce the Bakers' attitude as primitive: "You can't let people use ancient writings to derive dubious moral claims and then impose them on other people. If Christianity has any place in today's world, it lies in fostering love for all. Why don't these people reflect on the Parable of the Good Samaritan—and bake the cake?" Each style of external verdict has something going for it. That's the problem.

The case goes through the courts, and the law eventually decides. Perhaps the final judgment compels the making of a cake, on pain of violating laws against discrimination on grounds of sexual preference. As a result, the Bakers—as well as many other members of their church—are aggrieved, wounded in their pursuit of service to the Lord (as they conceive it), deprived of their freedom, and alienated from their nation's culture. Or perhaps the law allows the Bakers' refusal to stand. George and Ed—together with other members of the LGBTQ community and with all people who have celebrated the increasing acceptance of same-sex love—see in the decision a renewal of the disgust and loathing that has blighted the lives of homosexuals in the past, another instance of irrational prejudice and primitive superstition. The long battle isn't over.

Progressive Mill favors neither of these outcomes.

⨍

Let's imagine a different ending to the story. George, Ed, and the Bakers have a mutual friend, Jessica. Learning what has occurred, she offers to mediate. "There's no need for conflict or coercion," she says, "this can be worked out." At first, everyone is dubious. But Jessica has attained an empathetic understanding of both points of view, and that enables her to bring them all together. She arranges face-to-face conversations, initially in her presence, later without her. All those involved start to recognize one another as *people*, to comprehend why they adopt the stances they do, and, here and there, seeds of sympathy are planted.

And attitudes change. The Bakers are still influenced by the prohibitions of Leviticus, but it becomes harder for them to see George and Ed as wanton sinners flouting the divine law. Aspects of the men's relationship strike them as eerily familiar, resembling their own loving marriage. What George and Ed do in bed (or in some other private place) is wrong, an offense to the Lord, but it is not the perverse defiance they had taken it to be. They are moved by the potential parallel between these men and the wounded Samaritan, an outcast in his own age. They are touched by some of the incidents of ostracism and persecution George and Ed relate. Baking the cake now has two faces. On the one hand, it would be devoting their work to supporting a grievous sin. On the other, it would be an act of compassion, expressing Christian love for two people, admirable in some respects despite all their sinful conduct. They would minister to people who have been wounded by the world.

Analogously for George and Ed. Although they continue to think the Bakers' version of Christianity misguided, too narrow and rigid, too willing to subordinate morality to crude interpretations of peripheral parts of the Bible, they recognize the dedication and sincerity of the Bakers' faith. Moreover, as the conversations develop, the moments of connection become clearer. George and Ed observe how the Bakers have begun to see them as human beings, not as bestial sinners. Appreciating changes in the Bakers' perception of them, they can move beyond their own original judgment of their interlocutors as pious monsters.

Two emails cross. The one from George and Ed abandons the thought of a new battleground on which the next stage in the progress of freedom for gays must be fought; they volunteer to go elsewhere for their cake. The message from the Bakers reiterates their discomfort at baking the cake. But it also acknowledges what they have learned from the conversations. They confess to having been moved by what they have heard. Perhaps a compromise is possible? Their shop typically contains a few cakes George and Ed might find suitable, not specifically created for any wedding but easily adaptable. Maybe George and Ed would like to buy one of these and ask someone else to add the finishing touches . . . ?

When the messages are read, there's laughter in both houses. Jessica settles the issue by flipping a coin.

Surely a fantasy. This could never happen for many (or any?) of the serious instances in which human freedoms conflict. Yet the story suggests a direction in which to go, a potential way of making progress with respect to such clashes. Progressive Mill would approve of that direction.

The idea of autonomy, of choosing "your own good," already moves away from the thought of some external standard to which human lives ought to conform. To be sure, an objective constraint remains: the choice should be made by beings with "fully developed faculties," emotional and cognitive. The best an *individual* can do is to work out what is valuable and worthwhile through a process of *sensitive reflection*.

When individual decisions prove to conflict with one another, a *society* is faced with similar choices: a "good resolution" must be found. Just as a single person might subordinate the process of choice, appealing to an external standard, so, too, society might invoke some fixed body of principles. Yet the obvious analogue of Mill's procedure for the individual is to proceed differently at the social level, for those whom the clash affects to engage in *sensitive reflection*—together. That's what Jessica helps George, Ed, and the Bakers to do.

Progressive Mill would favor an embryonic methodology for addressing the tensions that arise when people pursuing their own good live side by side. There should be dialogue and joint deliberation. All the affected parties must be included (or, in cases of group conflict, there must be representatives of all perspectives). The discussions and negotiations should draw on "fully developed cognitive faculties": they should be well informed and cogently argued. Moreover, they should draw on "fully developed emotional capacities": participants should be mutually engaged, willing, even eager, to enter into others' perspectives, to try to see the world through their eyes and feel it in their skins, and aiming at a resolution all can accept.

Just as an individual's attempts to choose the good will likely be imperfect, so too for the social analogue. On both levels, the task is to make progress. To make individual people better able to reflect and to be sensitive. To make social decisions about conflicts over freedom more inclusive, better informed and better reasoned, more sympathetic and open to others. Very probably, no society will ever attain freedom for all. Progressive thinkers hope to improve the distribution of "the only freedom which deserves the name."

Skeptics will deny the possibility of advancing in this way. They may echo Frederick Douglass, claiming that "struggle," even violent struggle, is required for progress. Indeed, the history of human liberation has often witnessed the oppressed and dispossessed wrenching power into their own hands. That history has also been dependent on lucky contingencies; has involved massive waste, suffering, and death; and has been plagued by brutal reversals.

Mill, the progressive, thinks human societies can do better. A pragmatist at heart, he encourages us to try to make the future struggles for freedom less chancy and less bloody than they have hitherto been.

3

Democracy in Danger?

E legies for the demise of democracy are everywhere these days. The causes for lamentation are diverse. Some mourners point to the effects of gerrymandering, cunningly devised to promote minority rule. Others see the principal ill as lying in voter suppression, allegedly introduced to ensure the integrity of the ballot but designed to skew the vote in a particular direction. Yet others believe these troubles pale in comparison with the increasing disdain for constitutional guarantees and the flouting of written (and unwritten) norms. Many would agree that, behind the symptoms of democracy's decline, lies the radical polarization of the electorate. When fellow citizens come to be seen as enemies, more hateful even than some traditional national foes, political parties feel they must discard all restraints in the interest of gaining or retaining power. Moreover, the anger and spite directed against the opposition sometimes inspire a movement to abolish the claim to co-citizenship. Longstanding unions dissolve. Separatists campaign for withdrawal into a more congenial polity. That style of "solution" rightly arouses concern at a time when global issues require concerted international action.

Although prominent thinkers in the ancient world were critical of government by the people, the reputation of democracy in the past two centuries has been far more positive. Perhaps that assessment rests on the perceived awfulness of the competitors: in Winston Churchill's often misquoted remark, "It has been said that democracy is the worst form of Government except for all those other forms that have been tried from time to time." But what exactly is democracy's appeal?

Plato (no fan) knew the answer: the promise of freedom.

—◦∞∞◦—

The surface of democracy, as practiced today, displays an iconic act. On election day, voters head to the polls, complete ballots expressing their preferences among candidates, and submit their choices. How does this (often inconvenient and sometimes burdensome) conduct advance "the only freedom which deserves the name"?

Cynics might say: hardly, if at all. Yet, even if in most elections the citizens feel the candidates they choose to be only loosely connected with their most central aspirations, even if they think their vote will be swamped by a mass of others, the ballot box seems to offer some protection to their ability to "pursue their own good in their own way." They benefit from the shelter offered by their nation's constitution and its framework of basic laws. Were some political leader to endanger their attempts to attain what most matters to them, revoking a law on which secure pursuit of their good depends, they could combine to defeat the interference in their lives. Democracy promotes freedom by serving as a bulwark against threats. The votes people actually cast may have no impact on how well their lives go.

Nevertheless, democracy is valuable in guarding them against renewed unfreedom.

This conception of democracy as shield must face the challenge on which many of democracy's detractors have fastened. It presupposes an ability to *recognize* situations in which freedom is endangered. A long tradition, perhaps stemming from Plato, regards the masses as too unintelligent to develop that capacity. That is an elitist error. A related point, however, is equally troublesome. Intelligent people are often poorly informed on many issues. Ignorance can be as toxic as alleged native stupidity. Why should we think that citizens will always perceive where their interests lie and thus be able to detect incipient forms of tyranny?

Mill is often interpreted as advocating an answer to this question, one that would resolve it in principle but that fails in the rough-and-tumble contemporary world. As we shall see, he is less naïve than some of his readers take him to be, and his reflections on the issues involved indicate a line of response to the spate of epitaphs for democracy.

⸙

Chapter 2 of *On Liberty* is *the* classic discussion of free exchange of ideas. Like John Milton before him, Mill takes a free press to play a key role in disseminating truth. In the free and open arena where ideas engage one another, truth will win, enabling the spectators, whether in the luxury boxes or the bleachers, to appreciate the victory. Mill elaborates the point by identifying four virtues of public debate. Open discussions may overthrow claims wrongly accepted as true; they may extend partial truths by adding elements previously overlooked; they may expose the grounds on which established doctrines rest; and they may revive long-adopted beliefs, preventing them from becoming inert pieces of dead dogma. These aspects of his argument are rightly appreciated. The virtues he singles out are genuine.

Nevertheless, it is hard to read his brief for free speech without detecting at least a whiff of utopian idealism. Mill appears very confident about the functioning of the arena. Error will typically be routed. No judges (or spinmeisters) will be needed to tell the onlookers who has won. He seems to imagine a central podium equipped with a first-rate microphone and sound system. One by one, decorously and courteously, the advocates of the various positions ascend and, with impeccable clarity, deliver their arguments. Scrupulously fair, they always acknowledge points made by their opponents. Nor do they ever interrupt one another or hog the microphone. Those who listen are attentive and able to understand what they hear and assess the merits of the rival presentations. Mill was, of course, deprived of any opportunity to watch cable news or to spend happy hours in internet chat rooms. The tone of this part of his essay suggests, however, that he wasn't a regular reader of the tabloids of his day, either.

Yet he was not so naïve as to think of the ideal of free discussion as easily implemented. Toward the end of chapter 2, Mill acknowledges pressures that distort the functioning of the arena. He recognizes how free discussion can exacerbate polarization ("sectarianism"). People "of narrow capacity" can see no truth but their own belief, they become "impassioned," and the result is a "collision of opinions." Perhaps optimistically, he assumes that passions (sometimes "violent") won't infect the "more disinterested bystander" who will judge the intemperate performances.

In his conclusion, he gestures (vaguely) toward ensuring that "the manner be temperate" by setting "bounds of fair discussion." These baby steps toward acknowledging the potential erosion of his four virtues as the marketplace of ideas becomes dominated by intellectual thuggery are surely inadequate to the problems generated when media sources answer above all to considerations of profit, when "sectarianism" is prepared to wallow in "alternative facts" and to lambast opponents for the forms of turpitude it practices hourly. It is easy to patronize Mill for his ingenuousness, his pretty picture of a civilized world in which public debate is honest and polite. He is irrelevant, it seems, to the way we live now.

But that appearance is deceptive. Although *On Liberty* is hopeful (too hopeful) that a democracy committed to free speech will generate an informed electorate full of citizens who can perceive where their interests lie, other writings reveal how Mill appreciates the difficulties in achieving this state of widespread enlightenment. *Considerations on Representative Government* recognizes how difficult it is, not just for ordinary people but for their elected representatives, to understand the details of complex issues. Moreover, Mill freely admits the trouble leaders have experienced in aligning preferences (and consequent conduct) with their interests, and he does not expect ordinary citizens (the "labouring classes") to do better in this regard. Informed selections at the ballot box cannot reasonably be expected. Yet, he tells us, governments "must be made for human beings as they are, or as they are capable of speedily becoming." Given the real likelihood of the citizens' failure to identify what is good for them—and what might cause them fundamental harm by removing the protections on which their pursuit of the good depends—democracies, just as any other form of government, are subject to the danger that citizens will be hoodwinked by "the holders of power." How can a society "provide efficacious securities against this evil"?

Mill's approach to this question leads him to a form of elitism that angers some of his readers, indeed that provokes them to dismiss him altogether. Appalled by the potential tyranny of ignorance—an arrangement under which the badly informed outvote the smaller group of citizens with enlightened views—he recommends a "balanced" electorate, in which the votes of the two classes are roughly equal. The well-educated minority is to be given the same electoral weight as the "labourers," a group including all those who receive only minimal education. There are remnants of democracy, here. Mill does not want to suppress the voices of the masses entirely and to institute a managerial regime in which the experts decide (a position taken a few decades later, in the American context, by Walter Lippmann). He opts for awarding "plural votes" to the elite. Citizens are to be tested, with those demonstrating "superior function" being assigned two (or more?) votes. As Mill takes pains to point out, his hierarchy is no aristocracy, but meritocratic: "I consider it an absolutely necessary part of the plurality scheme, that it be open to the poorest individual in the community to claim its privileges, if he can prove that, in spite of all difficulties and obstacles, he is, in point of intelligence, entitled to them." Presumably, the system is to be organized and the number of votes granted to the elite determined so as to bring about the desired balance. If n people pass the "superior function" test and m fail, then the elite are given r votes, where $nr = m$. (That formula for the political arithmetic underlying Mill's regime allows for the charming prospect that, when public education really succeeds, producing a majority of the "highly functional," the plural votes switch to the uneducated minority.)

Anyone sensitive to the ways that IQ tests have sometimes been used to justify distinguishing two classes of people will cringe at Mill's proposal. What kinds of questions will figure on the test he envisages? Will they be socially skewed, as historically many life-determining examinations have been? Even if concerns about "the mismeasure of man" are set on one side, there are powerful reasons to think the program inadequate to the task for which it is intended. For, in a society as complex as the one he knew—or the ones in which contemporary citizens make their electoral decisions—it's not obvious that any individual, let alone any sizeable group, can claim expertise on more than a tiny percentage of the issues to be resolved. So many questions arise, and so many of them turn on technicalities!

Mill might concede that walking encyclopedias are rare. But knowledge is not what he plans to measure. His concern lies with *intelligence*—and that, he points out, is the concept he employs to frame his discussion. But why should he have faith in any correlation between intelligence and level of education—either in nineteenth-century Britain or in twenty-first-century America? Furthermore, why should the awarding of plural votes to the intelligent guard against the mistaken choices he is concerned to avoid? Presumably, the intelligent *who devote themselves to a particular issue* are more likely to select a better policy *for that issue* than the many who make up their minds without significant thought. If all the intelligent choose the *same* issue on which to concentrate their mental powers, their use of the plural vote may offer the desired balance for that specific question. They will lack the time to dedicate themselves to the many other policy decisions needing to be made. So, on the overwhelming majority of the issues, they will be in no better position than the *Lumpenproletariat* with their single votes. If, on the other hand, the questions are divided up among the plural voters, none of the issues will be guided by the informed judgments of more than a handful of the intelligent. Hence, for any decision, the outcome will be determined by the uninformed, and the balance Mill aims for will not be attained.

Unless, of course, the intelligent agree in advance that, with respect to any issue, they will all follow the lead of that subset of their members who have focused on the question. Then the proposed system has a chance of working as planned. But why stop there? If plural votes are to be cast by committed deference to designated authorities, why not make the system fully general? Instead of risking the possibility that the uninformed votes of the masses will override the decisions on which their colluding superiors have agreed, wouldn't it be preferable to propose extending the rule of expertise? No need for the division into two classes. Across the entire society, individuals (or groups of individuals) become designated experts on particular questions. Based on their particular experiences (not on the devotion of powerful minds to study an issue), even agricultural laborers and miners can claim expertise on some matters. Voting drops out of the picture. The society chooses whatever the experts recommend.

In attempting to protect democracy against ignorance, Mill opens a door. On the other side, waiting to congratulate him, is

Walter Lippmann. "Well done," he says, "you have recognized that democracy presupposes the omnicompetent citizen; as you have begun to see, there can be no such character. Welcome to the managerial society."

⸺

Mill's tendencies to favor hierarchies based on what he takes to be merit stem from his commitment to human progress. He is haunted by the thought of advances being derailed through foolish decisions made by people whose deliberative capacities have not yet developed to the level required to resolve the issues confronting them. His alarm surfaces in the proposal to amend democracy by awarding plural votes to the section of the electorate he sees as likely to make the wisest choices. It emerges elsewhere, too.

On Liberty is very clear on the importance of interfering with someone's conduct, even when it would adversely affect only that person, if the individual has not yet reached the appropriate level of maturity. Parents rightly intervene in the early years of their children's lives. Mill does not question the exercise of "absolute power" during "the whole period of childhood and nonage." Moreover, what goes for people applies to whole societies, too. The imperative of noninterference lapses in "those backward states of society in which the race itself may be considered as in its nonage." That brief remark isn't specific enough to raise the typical reader's blood pressure. *Considerations on Representative Government*, however, is quite another matter.

Mill's defense of colonialism is qualified. He regards as "vicious" any policy of ruling nations for purposes of economic exploitation. In its past domination of some parts of the world largely populated by British emigrants—he has Canada and Australia in mind—England, he charges, behaved "like an ill brought-up elder brother." Progress was made when Great Britain allowed full self-governance to "her colonies of European race." Nevertheless, there are occasions on which nations are right to govern distant regions of the world. India, a country to whose administration Mill devoted many years, is his prime example.

Predictably, his defense of colonial rule is high-minded. The (benevolent) work must be done in the interests of human progress. Intervention is wrong when countries are "capable of, and ripe for, representative government." It is entirely justified, when they, "like India, are still at a great distance from that state."

However high-minded the motivating principle, that sentence rightly strikes many people as crass. Who is Mill or the East India Company or the British government to dismiss an ancient culture, with its own rich traditions, with a glancing declaration that it's not yet ready for what remote and uncomprehending observers view as the ideal form of government? Reactions to Mill's sentence (and its further elaboration in the chapter in which it occurs) are sometimes extreme. Historians and anthropologists of my acquaintance snort at the mere mention of Mill and refuse to see any merit in his writings. For them, that large blind spot is enough to block appreciation of his ideas and arguments on any question.

Mill's factual judgment about the "maturity" of India is an insensitive blunder. His assumption that nineteenth-century British democracy was sufficiently advanced to serve as a pattern for all nations was, at best, dogmatic and uncritical. Even the principle itself, with its goal of helping very different societies develop, invites dangerous and ill-founded applications, and the analogy between the nonage of children and the nonage of nations is far from straightforward. Human infants are helpless, and, as they grow, they need sensitive and attentive guidance if they are to find their way to "their own good" and to enjoy "the only freedom which deserves the name." An ideal education must listen for the individual voice and help it express its own song—as the passionate defense of individuality in chapter 3 of *On Liberty* and as the *Subjection of Women* essay's even more passionate condemnation of ignorant imposition of social roles both appreciate. What features of a different nation warrant any judgment of parallel developmental stages? To be sure, countries struck by natural disasters may benefit from a helping hand, one that bestows the material resources they lack, but they are not, as very small children are, incapable of making their own use of what they are given. Sometimes, of course, their leaders may do abominable things, violating human rights and moral principles—and a large part of the populace they lead may even approve. When that occurs, external pressure or even direct intervention can be justified, in order to protect the potential victims. None of this supports regarding the societies in question as so backward in their development as to need the benevolent rule of others. The diagnosis of "nonage" pretends to identify a general condition, one that demands intervention across the board, not outside efforts at ameliorating some particular aspects of its current state.

So Mill's brief for "enlightened colonialism" goes badly astray. It is radically at odds with the individualism at the core of *On Liberty* and with the arguments he offers in favor of the political freedom of women. Yet, as I shall suggest, there are elements, even in this rightly criticized part of his work, that prove useful in attending to the problems besetting democracy.

⸺⸎⸺

Progressivist Mill celebrates individuality. Political freedoms, the ability to vote, for example, or the opportunity to engage in free debate, deserve their status because they foster in citizens the power to seek their own good. Informed by the "experiments of living" earlier generations have tried, benefiting from the customs they have inherited but not confined to imitating the past, they must work out for themselves their own "plans of life." For this, they will require the full development of their "faculties." As we might expect, given his reflections on his own history, Mill takes these faculties to include "discriminative feeling." He is explicit in not limiting development to the purely cognitive: "Desires and impulses are as much a part of a perfect human being, as beliefs and restraints." The political organization of a society is judged by its capacity for allowing the full development of its citizens. It is to cultivate individuality.

In doing so, it must harmonize the aspirations of different people. Democracy is promising in this regard, since a democratic society can provide a shield against the "encroachments" of the "stronger specimens of human nature." That is something, but it is surely too little for Mill's progressive purposes. A world in which negative freedom is perfected—one in which each individual is assured of noninterference from others—is completely compatible with abject failure in promoting the full development of the faculties and a genuine choice among experiments of living. Imagine a contemporary society in which the operations of the law are efficient, unprejudiced, and uncorrupted. The poor child from the ghetto can walk to school without fear. The neighborhood is carefully monitored, and violence is nipped in the bud. Nevertheless, the child is often too hungry to concentrate, the places called "home" change with enormous rapidity, and the school is staffed by weary teachers who have abandoned all hopes of conveying much to their pupils. Although, occasionally, some ability to find an individual path may emerge, it's reasonable to think such cases will be infrequent.

Mill requires more of democratic societies than the features I have listed: votes, elections, constitutional guarantees, free exchange of ideas, and an informed electorate (one that doesn't betray its own central projects in casting the ballot). Not only must he solve the problem of electoral ignorance and find a remedy for "sectarianism" (polarization) and overheated public debates, but he must also foster full development of cognitive and emotional capacities and arrange for harmonious coordination of the individual plans of life. It is a tall order.

Nevertheless, passages in his writing indicate a direction for deepening democracy. A useful clue comes from the misguided account of how immature nations might emerge from their nonage.

―――∞―――

Mill's benign colonialist is an educator. This teacher is extremely concerned to help in the advance of the nation he administers. Unfortunately, however, he seems not to have read chapter 3 of *On Liberty* or much of *The Subjection of Women*. For, rather than taking individuality seriously, he sees himself as leading the immature polity to a goal he, in his wisdom, can prescribe in advance. He has missed Mill's striking declaration that political tyranny may sometimes be preferable to apparently liberal regimes that force lives to conform to fixed patterns: "Even despotism does not produce its worst effects, so long as individuality exists under it; and by whatever name it may be called, and whether it professes to be enforcing the will of God or the injunctions of men." To which might be added: "and the individuality of a nation is squashed when the injunctions of men aspire to impose a system of government they regard as superior to all others." He has also failed to register Mill's bitter skepticism about whether "any man, or all men taken together, should have knowledge which can qualify them to lay down the law to women as to what is, or is not, their vocation." Or, at very least, he has been blind to an obvious parallel.

Progressive Mill views the proper development of individual people as proceeding differently from the treatment of individual nations favored by his colonial would-be educator. Crucial to the shaping of the growing person is the preservation and expansion of the subject's autonomy. As we saw in the previous chapter, autonomy is a matter of degree. The choices of a fully grown person have inevitably been molded to some extent by external factors—the horizon within which someone chooses is inevitably bounded by the possibilities the ambient culture can envisage. Despite that banal fact, autonomy can be expanded or contracted by the way in which education has been conducted. Those who teach the growing child need not behave like domineering theatrical directors—or Mill's colonial administrator—casting their charges into fixed roles and insisting on specific ways of playing the parts.

Yet, as the discussion in chapter 2 argued, there is no pre-formed self to be drawn out through sensitive socialization. Another great champion of individuality, Friedrich Nietzsche, offers a useful image. We should not think of proper socialization as eliciting the innate features of the embryonic person: true education, Nietzsche tells us, is a kind of freeing; the seeds of the mature individual are permitted to grow, protected from the weeds, rubbish, and pests that would interfere with their development. Armed with an understanding of genetics and development unavailable either to Mill or to Nietzsche, we can extend the metaphor. The traits of plants are not literally present in the seeds. Nor, except for the grossest features, is any specific characteristic determined to emerge in every possible environment. (To make the point crudely: treat your seedlings harshly enough, and they will die.) What we view as healthy growth is based not on our understanding of what is in the seed but on the absence of what we can identify as inhibiting agents: poor soil, too much or too little water, as well as the noxious interferences Nietzsche mentions. In the human case, failures to provide a rich menu of options for the young serve as obvious analogs of poor soil and bad watering; the stereotypes ("You're a girl, so you shouldn't expect to be good at math!") and the coercions ("No, that's wrong—you have to do it this way!") are the equivalents of the weeds and the pests.

Attentive gardeners watch for signs of health or sickliness. Attentive teachers, concerned to promote individuality, will focus on the directions in which the nascent person is tending. Good education, like good gardening, depends on the character of the process. The individuality Mill hopes to cultivate depends on a sensitive dialogue between those who form the young and their pupils. Sensitivity is not a matter of imposing patterns or shouting commands. It is, first and foremost, a matter of listening.

—∞∞∞—

With respect both to individual citizens and to nations, Mill takes progress to come through an education that develops capacities more fully than has been achieved in the past. In the case of nations, he forgets his most fundamental commitments in the interest of defending colonialism. When he considers citizens, the sin is one of omission. He does not elaborate his insights to propose a cure for the ills of democracy (some of which, as we have seen, he recognizes clearly). The elements, however, are there. I shall try to bring them together, thereby constructing what progressive Mill ought to have said.

In discussing the role of expertise in a democracy, Mill advocates a division of labor. Administration, he tells us, requires a single leader, someone who has deep knowledge of the pertinent issues and who can issue consistent and unambiguous directives. Yet the voices of the people must be heard. Assemblies of citizens have a crucial role to play: "What can be done better by a body than by any individual is deliberation. When it is necessary, or important to secure consideration to many conflicting opinions, a deliberative body is indispensable."

The growth of the polity is shaped by the interactions among citizens, by exchanges of ideas among representatives of the various perspectives among the electorate. One of the problems for Mill's version of democracy is that of harmonizing the various plans of life. Since even the most gregarious person is unlikely to know the aspirations of all those who will be potentially hampered by the pursuit of that person's own life plan, conflicts are inevitable. To avoid "encroaching" on one another, fellow citizens will have to modify their own projects, to reshape the ways they pursue their own good. *Mill does not see this as something to be regretted.* What is given up is compensated: "Even to himself there is a full equivalent in the better development of the social part of his nature, rendered possible by the restraint put upon the selfish part. To be held to rigid rules of justice for the sake of others, develops the feelings and capacities which have the good of others for their object."

These sentences are often overlooked by readers who think of Mill's individuals as thoroughly isolated, composing in their protected spaces their plans of life, and only needing highly developed cognitive capacities to do so. (Interpretations of this style are easily understood—many passages in Mill's writings are compatible with them.) For those who recall the close of the St. Andrews address, with its exhortation to the students to leave their "fellow creatures some little better for the use" they have made of their educations, what he says here should come as no surprise. Nor to anyone who reflects on Mill's life and on his discovery of the importance of interpersonal relations.

Our education continues beyond our schooldays, apparently, in the growth of fellow feeling, in the sacrifices we—willingly!—make as we find out how what we have aspired to would inhibit others, and in our revisions of our plans of life to resolve the conflicts. On Mill's account, democratic assemblies not only smooth the jagged edges where individual projects collide. They also educate and thereby refine "the only freedom which deserves the name." Deliberative democracy, as Mill conceives it, should be education.

From that flows a model for democracy, one promising to address its various ills. Education, recall, should proceed through a delicate dialogue. If individuals are to grow as Mill thinks they ought, deliberations with fellow citizens are properly guided by efforts to amend the indelicacies of the current versions. Those deliberations will be inadequate if perspectives, held by some of the populace, go unrepresented. They will be compromised if participants make claims at odds with the available evidence, or if they stick to claims they cannot justify, or if they stop the conversation with a table-thumping declaration. Above all, they will not achieve their purpose if they flout the norms of true education: if the deliberators fail to listen to the perspectives of all, to feel the world through others' skins, or to strive for an outcome with which all can live.

So we return to the embryonic methodology outlined at the conclusion of the previous chapter. *Deep* democracy institutionalizes deliberation, forms assemblies of citizens on issues over which there is conflict, and strives to make progress by solving three types of deficiency. The conversation should be as inclusive as possible. It should rely on the best available information. And it should aspire to the kind of mutual engagement found in the most sensitive educational settings.

Progressive Mill sees that species of deep democracy as addressing the problems found in shallower democratic ventures. But how exactly?

———— ✸ ————

First, by countering the trend to a polarized electorate. Demonization of those with whom we disagree is far less common when opponents talk face to face. Outpourings of spiteful invective on the internet are fueled by the anonymity of the medium. By contrast, when people of divergent views are asked to plan together, they can frequently find a modus vivendi. The calming of tempers is likely to be amplified if there are explicit and well-publicized norms for deliberating together. Awareness of what is expected often changes conduct. Almost everybody knows that exuberance at a funeral is frowned upon. That common knowledge checks the conduct of even the most boisterous people.

In a society where all citizens are regularly asked to participate in deliberations with others who hold very different perspectives and to engage with one another, the experiences can be expected to break down stereotypes of political opponents and to revive a sense of solidarity that transcends party lines. The effect can be further augmented if the education of the young is directed toward instilling a sense of fellow citizenship. This is inculcated not simply by regaling children with happy stories of the nation's history but through programs of joint student planning, starting in the early years in simple ways ("What game should we play?") and progressing to far more complex exercises, ones anticipating the divisions of political life and including an ever expanding diversity among the participants. Educators can try to prepare the developing citizens for their future role as democratic deliberators.

How far can that go? Until experiments are tried, nobody can be sure. Perhaps there would be only a modest reduction of fierce and unyielding partisanship. Yet some trials have been conducted, and the results are promising. A Canadian citizens' assembly, held in 2004 in British Columbia, crafted a proposal for reforming electoral law, and, in 2016, a similar group in

Ireland deliberated about whether to repeal the eighth amendment to the constitution, which banned abortion as illegal; after receiving (and discussing) input from thousands of Irish citizens, it concluded by voting 79 to 12 in favor of repeal. As the possibility of achieving consensus—probably rough and incomplete, especially at first—comes to be appreciated, the common conception of those "on the other side" as pathological evildoers can be expected to fade.

As it does, the pressures driving the familiar moves to distort democracy will lessen. Why try to ensure that your party draws the boundaries of political districts, when the history of democratic deliberation reveals that a bipartisan group can reach agreement? Why insist that your people (and only your people) count the votes, if experience shows that integrity isn't the possession of any single political sect? Why turn up the temperature in vituperative debates, when you have learned how to have calm and productive conversations about political differences?

So far, the hardest issue of all, the problem driving Mill to offer special status to the educated (and "intelligent"), remains unaddressed. No fruitful deliberation without well-grounded information. How are inexpert citizens, with various levels of education, to acquire the factual information they need to make headway with the issues they confront? The obvious answer: they can consult experts, who will tutor them (recall Mill's division of labor). All well and good, but, as has become blindingly obvious, in today's world different constituencies hail different people as authoritative. When that occurs, our deliberators have no option except to engage in joint inquiry. They must be prepared to expose their reasons for making the attributions of authority they do, and they must assess together the evidence for a putative expert's reliability. For this to succeed, the mutual engagement of the deliberators is essential. Discussions are frequently stymied by the fear that if some people are accepted as authoritative, a particular conclusion will follow, and, as a result, the lives of those drawn to alternative "experts" will be devastated. The solidarity and sense of fellow citizenship required to protect each member of the society is lacking. Thus, with a sense of their own vulnerability, those threatened by the designation of particular people as experts will resist to the end.

Philosophers, as well as many others, are beguiled by a faulty picture. Ethical and political deliberation should settle the facts first and, on this basis, inquire into questions about value. Too simple. One ethical/political commitment must be in place before joint inquiry can begin. Whatever the outcome, each citizen's well-being must be protected. Only when that becomes common knowledge can deliberations work their way out of the thicket of "alternative facts."

It would be folly to view these remarks as a full defense of the power of Mill's "deep democracy" to cure all democracy's ills. They are best seen as pointers in a direction it would be profitable to explore. Self-described realists will surely be skeptical, accusing me (if not Mill) of a rosy vision based on unsupported hopes. Is the quest for revival of fellow citizenship quixotic?

That question cannot, should not, be answered without experimentation—without "experiments of living together" (to adapt a Millian phrase). Skeptics are held by the vision of political opponents who view one another so sourly that any discussion among them will quickly degenerate into a chorus of snarls. It would surely be a bad strategy to begin with the most unbending advocates of a particular perspective. Better to select those who, while thoroughly committed to a point of view, are open-minded enough to want to listen to what can be said on the other side. If they can be brought into a fruitful conversation, the habit may spread (in stages) among their more adamant fellow travelers. Nor can anyone tell in advance what may be achieved by developing explicit norms for conversation, openly designed to allow all voices a hearing. Should the dialogue have a moderator, someone good at lowering the temperature? Should there be preliminary training, to cultivate habits of listening? Can an educational program grow future citizens who will be more inclined to open their ears to others' concerns?

The ventures in small-scale deliberative democracy that have been tried so far (two of which were mentioned earlier) do not provide any systematic answers to these questions. They offer, as I have said, encouragement: promoting solidarity is not entirely hopeless. Proliferating similar enterprises, and sometimes deliberately varying the conditions under which the participants exchange their views, might reveal differences in the fruitfulness of rival approaches. The future can build on these in attempts to go further.

Progressive Mill is a committed experimentalist—as is clear from his most conspicuous progressivist cause. In opposing "the legal subordination of one sex to the other," he confronts those who take the existing social relations among men and women to have emerged as the optimal possibility. His first objection questions the evidential basis for the claim: "The opinion in favor of the present system, which entirely subordinates the weaker sex to the stronger, rests upon theory only; for there never has been trial made of any other: so that experience, in the sense in which it is vulgarly opposed to theory, cannot be pretended to have pronounced any verdict."

The "realist's" skepticism about the possibilities of fellow citizenship is in the same position. Until the trials have been done, experience will not have "pronounced any verdict." Hence, Mill would ask, why not try for a desirable goal and see how far we can get?

4

Inevitable Inequality?

The drumbeat of shocking statistics goes on and on. The United States has greater wealth inequality than other affluent nations. Economic inequality has been increasing for the past four decades (with the period from 1998 to 2007 being especially significant). The net worth of the top 1 percent of American households is more than fifteen times that of the bottom 50 percent. A majority of American citizens find these figures disturbing. There is broad support for remedying the situation—even for redistributing wealth by raising tax rates on billionaires.

Yet there are loud voices, popular in some circles, who tell the world that "interfering with the free market" is a Very Bad Idea. The economic doldrums of the 1970s were cured by abandoning the follies of attempts at regulation, and, like many nations, the United States has benefited from a return to sanity. We should never have forgotten the lesson of classical political economy. Laissez-faire benefits everyone.

⸻

A myth—as many of the world's most eminent economists recognize. The completely unregulated market belongs with the tooth fairy and the Fountain of Youth. No market can perform its functions unless background conditions are in place. There must be a framework of laws to govern transactions and mechanisms for ensuring that they are obeyed. Otherwise, neither buyers nor sellers will take the risks involved in trying to exchange goods. There must be means of access to the sites where the exchanges occur, roads or canals or railways, vehicles and a complex system to assure safe travel, or (in our day) airplanes, shipping containers, and internet connections. There must be ways for potential customers to find out about commodities on offer. Maybe, to prepare them for doing so, they will have to be literate and numerate. So, there must be some minimal education.

Must the conditions be supplied by a central agency, by the intrusive state? Aficionados of the free market may propose privatizing the construction of the necessary infrastructure, only to find themselves trapped in a regress. For if the work is left to individual enterprise, it will involve transactions in another market (in which suppliers compete for the favors of potential consumers), and that market will require just the same background conditions. Indeed, allowing private ventures to play a role *increases* the number of sites at which regulation is required: now you have to supply laws to govern public action *and* private action—and to cover the interplay between them.

Alvin Roth's lecture on the occasion of winning the Nobel Memorial Prize in Economics provides a simple and lucid explanation of what "free" means in this context: "A free market is a market with rules and institutions that let it operate freely. When we talk about a wheel that can rotate freely, we don't mean a wheel that is unconnected to anything else. We mean a wheel that has an axle and well-oiled bearings." A principal theme of

Roth's lecture (and of his life's work) is that markets need to be *designed*. Wheels are typically set up with axles and bearings because people want them to do various jobs. Similarly, when we set up a market, it's important to think about what we intend it to provide.

The advocates of laissez-faire want to remove all the regulations they can. The "free market" they have in mind is the *minimally regulated* market. Why do they think markets should be designed that way? What exactly is the envisaged function?

If those questions were posed to them, they would probably wax lyrical about national prosperity and "making America great again." That's just bluster. There's one thing minimally regulated markets can achieve. They can be expected to deliver consumer goods at the cheapest prices, typically as a result of depressing wages, thereby increasing the wealth gap between the masses who contribute their labor and the few who run the show.

In the spirit of Roth's lecture, it seems right to ask: Is that the goal we want to achieve?

⸺⸺⸺

Progressive Mill (indeed, *any* defensible version of Mill) would answer with a resounding "No!" His conception of progress centers on the development of faculties to enable people to enjoy "the only freedom which deserves the name." The thinker who saw Bentham as overlooking the higher pleasures and who condemned him for seeing in human life "little but what the vulgarest eye can see" would be even more incensed at the reduction of human well-being to the amassing of material goods. Yet Mill belongs in the pantheon of the classical political economists. His *Principles of Political Economy* (roughly four times as long as

On Liberty and *Utilitarianism* combined) went through eight editions in his lifetime. That work contains a lengthy discussion of the merits of what he calls "*laisser-faire*," continued in the posthumously published *Chapters on Socialism*. Perhaps, then, he should be seen as deeply torn: a fellow traveler with today's free-marketeers, a thinker whose fundamental philosophical commitments are diametrically opposed to the functions minimally regulated markets can discharge?

No. Although there are tensions within Mill's thoughts about inequality, they take, as we shall see, a different form. His purely *economic* writings are pervaded by his judgments about what is most valuable in human life. Nor should that be surprising. The idea that the contemporary fetish for minimally regulated markets is the return to and renewal of classical political economy is another part of the myth. Any careful reading of *Wealth of Nations* reveals numerous places at which Adam Smith suggests interventions, often motivated by a concern for the welfare of the workers. To a lesser extent, Ricardo's economic program was shaped by the reformist ideas he shared with Bentham. Classical political economy was driven by the engagement of philosophical discussions of values with investigations in social science.

None of its practitioners (with the possible exception of Marx) pursued that engagement more thoroughly than Mill. Book 2 of his *Principles* has an astonishing title: "Distribution." According to prior orthodoxy, political economy has no need to consider how income and wealth may be distributed—the task is to understand how aggregate wealth is amassed and, consequently, how an economy can prosper in the work of accumulation. Once that is organized, the chips—the bullion and the banknotes—fall where they may. Given Mill's philosophical commitments, however, the aggregative approach is insufficient. "Each is to count as one and none for more than one"—that is a principle he applauded in Bentham and one he continues to espouse. Advancing beyond Bentham's narrow conception of human life, it is to be applied to the full development of individuals. Progress consists in promoting the growth of each, as far as is possible. Distribution of wealth gains its importance because Mill recognizes how lives of the kind he hopes to encourage require a material basis and that concentrations of wealth in the hands of the few will retard human progress. He anticipates Roth's point. Markets should be constructed to serve the ends we intend to achieve. Maximizing aggregate wealth without regard for distribution is a poor idea if the guiding ideal is the full development of each individual. For when the distribution is skewed, the vast majority of the population is consigned to a "puerile" state—and the few who wallow in luxury are, as Mill sees it, unlikely to enjoy lives "such as human beings with highly developed faculties can care to have."

So Mill proposes to regulate the economy in a very specific way. He will reform the laws of inheritance.

⸺⸺

Human beings, he contends, will inevitably differ in their talents and industry, and, in consequence, in each generation, some will become richer and others poorer. Nevertheless, the moments at which wealth passes across the generations allow the possibility of benign regulation:

> The inequalities of property which arise from unequal industry, frugality, perseverance, talents, and to a certain extent even opportunities, are inseparable from the principle of private

property, and if we accept the principle, we must bear with these consequences of it: but I see nothing objectionable in setting a limit to what any one may acquire by the mere favour of others, without any exercise of his faculties, and in requiring that if he desires any further accession of fortune, he shall work for it.

Evening out the distribution of wealth has two principal virtues. First, and most obviously, it provides a material basis to support the growth of individuals whose lives would otherwise be stunted by poverty. Second, it acts as a spur to people who would be awarded large legacies and, in consequence, fail to develop and exercise their talents.

Mill maintains that "enormous fortunes" are unnecessary: nobody needs them except for "ostentation or improper power." Moreover, he supposes them detrimental to those who receive them, sapping the will for personal growth. Nevertheless, his respect for private property inclines him to leave the redistribution in the hands of the rich (presumably when they draw up their wills). They are to decide in which directions their largesse will flow, subject only to the restriction that not too much of it can flow down any particular channel. His belief in the virtues of intergenerational redistribution rests on a conjecture: "A large portion also of the accumulations of successful industry would probably be devoted to public uses, either through direct bequests to the State, or by the endowment of institutions; as is already done very largely in the United States, where the ideas and practice in matters of inheritance seem to be unusually rational and beneficial." (Mill seems to foresee the coming of Andrew Carnegie but not the conception of all taxation as theft and the particular animosity directed against "death taxes.")

Perhaps his optimism rests on thinking of a deeply democratic society in which solidarity among citizens is well entrenched. Or does he stop short of requiring inheritance taxes to allow the rich to exercise a—nonfundamental—freedom?

The *Principles* is remarkable for another divergence from the political economy of his age. Economic thinking in the early nineteenth century had been haunted by a looming specter. (Not Marx's communism—that had not yet been born.) According to received theory, the period through which any economy could grow was necessarily finite. Sooner or later, the rate of profit would sink to zero, investment would wither away, and further growth would become impossible. The society would have reached the dreaded "Stationary State."

The most distinguished economists of the times wrestled with the problem of how to avoid or at least postpone this unfortunate condition. They assumed that growth was required for economic health (including, in particular, good wages for the workers—Adam Smith's "liberal reward of labor"). Mill, however, was an outlier. Not only was he unafraid of the stationary state; he welcomed it.

The limit to economic growth will be attained when technological improvements and exploitation of the planet's resources (and of the people who inhabit the hitherto "uncultivated and ill-cultivated regions of the earth") can go no further. When that happens, Mill asks, "In what condition are we to expect it will leave mankind?" His fellow economists had arrived at their gloomy prophesies by focusing on the depressed rate of profit and on its supposed economic consequences. Characteristically, however, Mill's own assessment is made on the basis of what he regards as most valuable in the human condition. If checks are in place to prevent population growth—if societies and individuals practice "restraint" in reproducing—he finds no reason for supposing the material bases of human life would have to be spread more thinly. The supply of resources to people is not, of course, an ultimate end. It is a means to their developing their individuality, finding their own good, and pursuing it in their own way. Why should that be negatively affected by the end of economic growth?

Indeed, the most obvious impact on human lives of a transition to the stationary state is the removal of aspects of present society that *interfere* with the abilities of many people to live well. *Benefits* come with the end of dog-eat-dog capitalism.

> I cannot, therefore, regard the stationary state of capital and wealth with the unaffected aversion so generally manifested towards it by political economists of the old school. I am inclined to believe that it would be, on the whole, a very considerable improvement on our present condition. I confess I am not charmed with the ideal of life held out by those who think that the normal state of human beings is that of struggling to get on; that the trampling, crushing, elbowing, and treading on each other's heels, which form the existing type of social life, are the most desirable lot of human kind, or anything but the disagreeable symptoms of one of the phases of industrial progress.

Attaining the stationary state would, Mill thinks, eliminate many of the factors currently inhibiting people from living well.

In line with his thoughts about proper distribution of material goods, he points to a positive change that might occur when urges to fierce competition are finally quenched: "The best state for human nature is that in which, while no one is poor, no one desires to be richer, nor has any reason to fear being thrust back by the efforts of others to push themselves forward."

Anyone who reflects on human progress, understanding the contemporary condition as a state that has not yet attained what really matters—the development of individual lives that go well—will "be comparatively indifferent to the kinds of economical progress which excites the congratulations of ordinary politicians." Mill's charges are as apt today as they were nearly two centuries ago. The measures on which economic advisors fixate are "in themselves . . . of little importance." No society should take great pleasure in learning that "persons who are already richer than anyone needs to be . . . should have doubled their means of consuming things which give little or no pleasure except as representative of wealth." The emphasis on increasing production is only justified "in the backward countries of the world." By contrast, "in those most advanced, what is economically needed is a better distribution."

A more equal distribution? Greater equality is one component in the reformed distribution Mill envisages. It must be accompanied by "a stricter restraint on population" (norms to check population growth). And it cannot be achieved simply by "levelling institutions." The goal is not simply to reduce the heights; we must "permanently raise the depths." In order to make progress in this way, Mill recalls his scheme for changing the laws of inheritance, and, in the present context, he offers more details about how the changes will improve human lives and human societies. Workers will be better paid (because some of the money will be directed to wage supplements?). The largest fortunes will have been built up in a single lifetime (avoiding the damaging effects on those born with chestfuls of silver spoons crammed into their mouths?). Far more importantly, it will create a larger number of people "with sufficient leisure, both physical and mental, to cultivate freely the graces of life, and afford examples of them to the classes less favourably circumstanced for their growth." On a charitable interpretation of progressive Mill, he may envisage a sequence of steps in which the very poorest groups are provided a secure material basis for their existence, while those who have already attained that are offered more time—and education?—to develop their own plans of life on the basis of more highly developed faculties and through the observation of a variety of "experiments of living." (We shall return to the character of Mill's egalitarian tendencies shortly.)

This remarkable discussion of the stationary state concludes with two further points. First, Mill warns against growing the human population and forcing human production to its theoretical limit. A world in which human beings could not enjoy solitude would be impoverished. Being alone "in the presence of natural beauty and grandeur, is the cradle of thoughts and aspirations which are not only good for the individual, but which society could ill do without." Progressive Mill is an environmentalist, urging us to retain ecological diversity and preserve the wilderness. So, he hopes, people "will be content to be stationary, long before necessity compels them to it."

His second point is related. The stationary state, he suggests, ought to promote "mental culture, and moral and social progress."

Much more time could be devoted to "the Art of Living"—and our understanding of how to live is likely to advance when "minds [cease] to be engrossed by the art of getting on." Technology would be pursued with a new motive, not out of a desire to increase private wealth but to generate its "legitimate effect, that of abridging labour." So inventions would bear their proper fruit. Rather than being used to make a few people vastly richer, they would "become the common property of the species, and become the means of improving and elevating the universal lot."

⸺⸱⸺

The man who wrote the parts of the *Principles* on which I have focused was, apparently, no libertarian. He envisaged regulations galore and state intervention on a massive scale. He would be entirely at home in the progressive political parties of many contemporary nations. Nor are the passages I have cited at odds with the rest of his economic writings. They simply make explicit attitudes underlying all of the *Principles*, and they are compatible with the late work Helen Taylor collected as the *Chapters on Socialism*. In comparing the two systems "at their best," Mill continues to prefer capitalism to "communism." (What he thinks of under the latter heading descends from early-nineteenth-century French socialism—Marx hasn't appeared on Mill's radar.) Yet his version of capitalism absorbs ideas originally introduced by self-described socialists. He favors moves to equalize wealth and supports proposals for workers' cooperatives. Progressive Mill is a social democrat or market socialist avant la lettre. He anticipates Roth's brief for designing markets to achieve goals whose value has been recognized by a prior thoughtful analysis—and, of course, he has done the analytic work himself. His commitment to humanism underlies the version of capitalism he espouses. Capitalism must wear a human face.

———— ❦ ————

As the discussion of inheritance reveals, Mill is prepared to tolerate ("bear with") some inequalities in the distribution of material resources. He sees the right to property as allowing variation in wealth to arise from differences in talent, industry, frugality, and, "to a certain extent," from opportunities—does the qualification express a willingness to engage in redistribution by taxing entrepreneurs who simply get lucky? The principal site for amending the variable outcomes of individual effort and success is, however, the interface between the generations, across which money flows. Whether it is redirected and rechanneled as a result of the choices of the donors or by the work of the state, what kinds of outcomes does Mill hope for?

The guiding ideal depicts a world where nobody wishes for more wealth than they have and there is no need for people to "push themselves forward." That would occur if the resources available to each person were sufficient for three conditions to be met. First, each individual would have as much opportunity as any other to develop the faculties required for a well-grounded choice of life plan. Second, the abilities of different people to exercise those faculties in "choosing their own good" would be equal. Third, the chances of successfully pursuing the chosen plan would be the same for all. Nobody, Mill included, can reasonably expect to reach a state in which the three conditions are satisfied. Nevertheless, they are useful as diagnostic tools for use in attempts to make ethical and social progress.

Mill's version of egalitarianism thus emerges as a scheme for reallocation of resources that takes the following form:

1. In intergenerational transfers, massive accumulation of wealth is prohibited.
2. Rich benefactors are required to spread their wealth so as to reduce the differences among some individuals in the next generation.
3. To the extent that decisions are made by a public body—for example, the government—they are guided by attempts to reduce three types of inequalities: in opportunities for development, in access to a range of life options, and in support for pursuing the life plan chosen. (Mill might well add a clause encouraging, or even requiring, some portion of the legacies to be publicly administered—for example, by imposing inheritance taxation.)
4. As the decisions are made sequentially, generation after generation, the initial distribution of resources across the population is expected to become more equal.

Under 2, the wealthy members of the older generation would designate the particular beneficiaries whose relative poverty they wished to alleviate. According to 3, public agencies would select people (presumably not usually those already benefiting from 2) who were also relatively deprived and attempt to improve their situations. They might do so by creating public goods: an obvious way to enhance the development of the young or to increase the menu of life options they can foresee as possibilities for themselves is to endow educational institutions from which an entire group can profit. Notice, however, that 3 doesn't stipulate which members of the less-well-off population are to be targeted or the particular *dimensions* of their freedom (their development, their choices, their pursuits) to be enhanced. As we shall see later, these are important lacunae in the scheme as I have reconstructed it.

———

How does Mill's program (under this interpretation) relate to other approaches to creating a more equal society? Demands for equality rightly provoke the question "Equality of *what*?"—and a common answer uses terms that echo Mill's. A very large number of people accept the ideal of equality of opportunity. Among them, a significant proportion would contend that, in their societies, the ideal has already been realized (at least to the extent that attaining it is feasible). On that basis, they would typically reject the clamor for further equalization. Does Mill's scheme collapse to this familiar position? Does he turn out to be a libertarian wolf in an egalitarian sheep's clothing?

No. His commitment to redistribution is grounded in thinking of the most basic opportunities as profoundly unequal. He enunciates it again and again, in arguing that many things must be done to yield genuine female equality. The thought is not only correct. It applies as well to other projects of liberation. Many states have provided a *formal* right to the opportunities Mill views as crucial for enjoying the freedom he regards as fundamental. Each child is given access to a school. No child is forced to undertake a designated role (as, for example, in caste systems). Yet whether the school will provide development of the deliberative faculties, cognitive and affective, is by no means guaranteed. And, even in the absence of overt coercion—when nobody dictates a career tanning hides or collecting garbage—the options among which the school-leaver has to choose may offer only drudgery at minimal pay.

The percentage of African American lawyers in the United States is less than half the percentage of Americans who are Black. For over two centuries, Black Americans have been able to practice law—in some states. Today, a teacher might reassure a young African American: "You, too, could become a lawyer, even a judge or a Supreme Court Justice." For many pupils, however, that would not be a realistic option. An example from the previous chapter points to the moral. The African American child, being raised by a single parent, often homeless, sometimes hungry, sent to a dangerous and underfunded school staffed by a rotating corps of disillusioned teachers, has the *formal* opportunity to realize dreams of giving eloquent speeches in a courtroom—but, even with determined effort, that outcome is improbable. A bit more likely, perhaps, for the white child, living in a declining area of the American heartland, where the schools are safer and the parental resources slightly greater. The chances increase dramatically for their counterpart, born to a professional couple, who have lavished attention from birth on and selected the place in which they live on the basis of its excellent schools. When such vast differences occur, to claim that equality of opportunity has been provided is to perpetuate a charade.

Mill's central focus on individuals and on their development is guided by Bentham's slogan: each is to count for one and none for more than one. The sums are to be done by adding on a different scale. Not by totting up the pleasurable and painful moments, not by checking the formal right to attend school, not even by logging the number of classroom hours. The measure that matters is the genuine chance for growth. So Mill insists on redistribution of resources; on public institutions for raising the quality of education "from the depths"; on investment to ensure a sufficient supply of dedicated and well-supported teachers, able to inspire and guide the young, in places that are welcoming and equipped to expand horizons.

This one example is mirrored in many others. In their teens, both the African American and the white child from the depressed small town abandon their earlier aspirations. They recognize the options for their lives as limited. Perhaps, leaving school, they make a final concerted effort to achieve the careers they want—and it crashes in failure. Or they settle for menial work at low wages and a life of lingering resentment. Or do they simply drift, finding moments of pleasure where they can, many of them the Benthamite pleasures Mill takes to be secondary— sex without love, highs from drugs or alcohol with lows to follow, vestiges of camaraderie in joining a gang?

Although many philosophers influenced by Mill think of plans of life as constructed at a single stage, in an episode of late-adolescent or early-adult self-determination, that is a fiction. Tolstoy knew better. One of the great insights of *War and Peace*, illustrated by the careers of the novel's central figures, is that it may take decades, even most of a lifetime, to discover who you are and what you hope to become. Thus my focus on the early segments of human lives and on the need for support to be given if Mill's goals are even partially to be obtained only covers the most obvious aspects of a general condition. For the less wealthy members of many societies, genuine equality of opportunity for development and for choosing and pursuing their "own good in their own way" requires a program of redistribution to help them at many stages of their lives.

Mill is thus an *ambitious* egalitarian, concerned with the *many* ways that resources need to be rechanneled if people are to have equal chances of enjoying the most important kinds of good.

───❦───

Or is he? Given his focus on individuality, he expects people to shape their lives in very different ways—and rejoices in that diversity. Projects, of course, vary in what is required to help them succeed. Universities, it is sometimes (unseriously) suggested, shouldn't invest in physicists, chemists, and biologists, all of whom need expensive equipment; mathematicians are cheap, completely set up when they have blackboards, chalk, and erasers; philosophers are cheaper still, since they can dispense with the erasers.

So, an objector may claim, it's wrong to cast Mill as an egalitarian. *Inequality* isn't the issue. *Insufficiency* is. Mill rightly recognizes how some members of society don't have enough, and he proposes to remedy the situation.

The objection, however, misses an important point. My plan of life is to write poetry—yours is to fathom the ocean depths. All I require is leisure, paper, and pencils, while your ventures demand extended voyages with plenty of costly equipment. In the Millian matching program, you are high maintenance, and I am a cheap date. Yet we should ask: How did we come by our chosen projects? If, from the outset, you were always showered with resources, given an education enabling you to explore a wide menu of options, whereas I was only given a training directed toward preparing me for menial work, then, in my reflective moments, I shall wonder if I selected my course *faute de mieux*. (I escaped a life of flipping burgers only because one of my early teachers detected an incipient talent for versifying.) Looking at your exciting life, I regard the horizons of my own early life as artificially narrowed. You could pick from a diverse array of possibilities. I could not. Perhaps, if I had had the chance, I too would have been an oceanographer. Or, turning the tables, *you* may have had the restrictive education—coerced by some extreme version of STEM into being trained only in technical subjects. So, coming to know me, you mourn your lost vocation as a poet.

The deepest discussions of poverty recognize that it has both an absolute and a relative dimension. To be poor is sometimes to lack enough to pursue your goals. Another type of poverty occurs when you have so much less than those around you that the goals you come to see as realistic options for yourself are far fewer than those to which your fellow citizens can aspire. You may have enough to do what you want (or tell yourself you want), but you reasonably wonder if those aims have been fixed by settling for less. For a thinker like Mill, the predicament is worrying. Choosing a plan of life is no simple matter. As he recognizes, the choice should be made by people with "fully developed faculties." The reflective people he has in mind will constantly review their choices—again exemplifying the Tolstoyan insight that finding yourself is a lifetime's work—and, as they do so, they will ask whether those earlier decisions were sufficiently informed (emotionally and cognitively) and were attuned to a sufficiently broad range of options.

The objector's mistake consists in starting too late. Mill's egalitarianism allows for variation in the delivery of support, since some projects are more demanding than others. At that stage egalitarianism consists in distributing resources so that everyone has roughly the same chances of success. Fixing that as the answer to the question "Equality of *what*?" depends, however, on supposing the choices to arise from opportunities to choose fully and widely—and, in that context, sufficiency can only be understood in terms of equality. Moreover, as *War and Peace* teaches us, that context isn't limited to an early phase of life but extends into full maturity.

———

It is time, however, to put Mill's egalitarianism to work and, in doing so, to expose the real tensions within it. Those arise from the vast gulf between the redistribution he would acclaim as ideal and the world he hopes to reform.

Ideals, I have suggested, should be viewed as diagnostic tools, alerting societies to current deficiencies and marking out directions in which they might do better. The egalitarian scheme I have reconstructed would provide support for significant numbers of people, even in the most affluent societies and even in those among them where inequality is already less pronounced. Moreover, it might be directed in any number of ways, through public goods or through transfers of funds, to affect the development of faculties, or to expand the menu of options from which people can choose, or to support their pursuit of the goals they set for themselves. To think of all these interventions as being made is a ludicrous fantasy. So how exactly would Mill recommend going forward? Which individuals have priority? To which aspects of their current condition ought we to pay most attention?

Consider some rival schemes for promoting the progress Mill envisages. First, we might devote all our efforts in remediation to the poorest segment of society, trying to ameliorate the material conditions that most limit the development of impoverished children. Replace the decaying schools in the unhealthy environments. Provide public housing for all those unable to afford to rent an apartment. Set up nutritional centers to which the indigent could go to obtain food. Supplement whatever incomes the extremely poor have. Although I shall treat this as a single strategy, it could evidently be implemented in a variety of ways, depending on how these four types of interventions were weighted. I ignore these differences, since they are small in comparison with others.

A second scheme writes off the most depressed segments of society. It concentrates instead on elevating the condition of those who seem close to a threshold. Consider a particular class of citizens. It contains some people whose current development is spotty or incomplete. Some aspects of their growth are as healthy as anyone's, but, in other respects, their faculties show defects. Others do fairly well across the board but are assessed as not quite ready for autonomous choice of a life plan. A third cluster consists of those who have made a reflective choice but whose pursuit of their goals always falls just short of success. Citizens in the class comprising these three types are close to the top of the "ladder of puerility," from which—with a little help—they could ascend to enjoy the kinds of lives Mill celebrates, those genuinely worth having. All resources are directed toward aiding them. (Once again, the scheme might be implemented in any number of ways.)

The third option focuses on the entire population. It considers a single institution, the educational system, "leveling up" so that every school in the nation succeeds, according to Mill's criteria, in delivering an education comparable to the best current examples. Teacher recruitment and training are radically expanded. All decrepit or unhealthy schools are replaced. Top-of-the-line equipment is distributed everywhere. One particular public good is equalized.

Which of these schemes would Mill take to be the best? His writings don't enable the question to be answered. Each of them is good in some respects and lacking in others. His theory of the good is not articulated in enough detail to allow a choice among them. Consider, for example, the relative merits of the first and second schemes. Should we always attend to the plight of those who are worst off (as the first would recommend) or direct our efforts toward raising people across the threshold so they can have lives of the kind a fully developed human being would care to have (the second scheme)? By Mill's lights, both goals are valuable. But he provides no principle we can use to decide which of them has priority.

And a good thing, too. When goods compete, when not everything worthwhile can be done, it is tempting to wish for some large piece of theory to be wheeled in to resolve the tension. In this instance, Mill's humanism is *rightly* conflicted. A sensitive moral agent *ought* to be torn. For it matters to those whose lives would be affected by one or the other scheme which of them is adopted. The tendency of morality and of moral philosophy is to envisage a complete moral system, one capable of being fathomed by people of sublime insight—illuminated by a deity, perhaps, or with a reason so highly refined as to recognize the moral law—a system offering answers to every moral question that may arise in any age. To my mind, a comprehensive and comprehensible moral theory of this kind is another myth. Progressive Mill frees himself from the hold of that myth.

How, then, would he decide whether the first or second scheme—or some compromise between them—should be the method of reform? *He* wouldn't—at least not without help from the potential targets of intervention. As the two previous chapters have suggested, to take autonomy seriously requires resolving conflicts by involving the parties affected. Jessica does not dictate to George, Ed, and the Bakers. She sets up conditions under which they can work through their differences. A polarized electorate requires institutions for doing the same on many scales. Democracy is rooted in conversations that strive to be inclusive, informed, and mutually engaged. The full theory of the good is not given in advance and applied to human situations. It emerges, situation by situation, from the ways people whose lives will be changed find a way of going on with which all can live.

The final chapter will say more about the picture of moral life I am attributing to Mill. Let's end this one by reflecting on a particular predicament, one in which considerations of inequality arise with overwhelming force—and one that presents the most important challenge of our times.

———

Our planet is heating up. Some of the consequences are already apparent: raging wildfires, prolonged droughts, unprecedented floods, frequent and powerful storms, life-threatening heatwaves.

Others are on the horizon: cascades of these events, uninhabit-
able regions, migration on a scale our species has never seen,
evolution of new disease vectors, pandemics. Nations have been
warned. Decades ago, the potentially harsh future was already
clear—and clearly explained. The responses have been pitiful:
refusals to accept the science, denial of human responsibility,
grudging acceptance, inadequate targets for reducing the emis-
sion of greenhouse gases, consistent failure to meet even the
unambitious goals that have been set. Small wonder many young
people fear the world in which they will grow old and in which
their children and grandchildren will grow up.

Why is climate action so hard? Because, as in the abstract
example of the previous section, it involves a many-sided
dilemma. Simplifying for present purposes, there are four worthy goals competing for resources:

1. Managing the transition to a habitable and sustainable
   planet
2. Attending to the plight of people within each nation
   whose lives are currently precarious
3. Helping developing nations attain the benefits the affluent
   world enjoys, without reliance on methods that would
   exacerbate global heating
4. Preserving the social, intellectual, and cultural achievements of the past

Around the world, the fearful young emphasize the first goal.
Within the affluent nations, especially those in which the distribution of wealth is grossly unequal, many poor people (and
the politicians who claim to represent them) resist the urgings

of climate activists, concerned that their programs would devastate their already difficult lives. Developing nations protest proposed curbs on emissions, charging (quite reasonably) that they should not have to pay (with suspended development) for the mess the industrial pioneers have created. Everybody agrees in principle with the importance of the fourth goal, but some are prepared to tinker with democracy ("Nations need a climate czar!"), and some are prepared to sacrifice "luxuries" (the arts, for example) to salvage the material resources future generations will need.

Even in this simplified picture, so many constituencies, each with an understandable perspective. What is to be done? Is there a cogent moral principle to balance the desiderata and resolve the conflict? Even if there is, would all the parties recognize it? Who, if anyone, would have the authority to enforce it? Is the idea of an enforcer itself morally suspect?

The best hope, I believe, is for the people—all the people—to speak, and to speak to one another. Our species needs a panhuman version of the kind of deliberation progressive Mill favors. Each constituency must be included in the conversation—future generations partially represented by the young but also by those best equipped to understand what coming environments will probably hurl at our descendants. Each committed to relying on the best available information. Each dedicated to finding not a perfect solution—there is none—but an outcome all can tolerate. A transnational citizens' convention on climate change. Happening now.

The details of the outcome cannot be foreseen (that's why the actual discussions are required!). Yet one prediction seems relatively safe. Without taking steps to remedy the inequalities of wealth, within nations and among them, no resolution is likely. Our future cannot afford "the trampling, crushing, elbowing, and treading on each other's heels" (individual and national) that would surely appall Mill if he observed the inhuman capitalism of our day. Part of the outcome must involve abandoning the kinds of markets in which myopic concern for gross and unnecessary profit dominates considerations of human well-being.

Mill tolerates intragenerational inequalities, products of the different trajectories of individual lives. Some inequality, he believes, is inevitable and will endure until the extinction of our species. He commends, however, reducing the fundamental inequalities, those affecting the quality of people's lives. If we fail to heed his calls for reform, the extinction of our species is likely to come sooner—far, far sooner—than he (or we) might reasonably have expected.

5

When Do the Numbers Count?

The mayor of a small town faces a decision. Funds are available for a new park, with a playground and fields for children's sports. Where should she put it?

A river bisects the town, dividing it into two regions inhabited by roughly the same number of people. The western half already has three parks, the eastern half only two. The decision seems obvious. The mayor should recommend to the Town Council that the park be placed in the east.

Our mayor is a *consequentialist*. She thinks the goodness or badness of a decision depends on the value of the outcome. Sometimes that can be settled on the basis of arithmetic. As, apparently, in the present instance. Two similarly sized populations, one with a one-park advantage over the other—put the new park in the under-parked area.

Perhaps she is also a *utilitarian*. She believes the arithmetic that counts assesses total happiness. Right actions are those producing the highest level of overall happiness. Happiness is increased as you raise the ratio of parks to children. That could be done by placing the park on either side. You get higher returns, however, when the starting ratio is lower. So adding an extra park to the two-park zone gives a bigger bang for the buck.

But she could be a different kind of consequentialist. An egalitarian, perhaps. What matters is producing a distribution of resources as equal as possible. Placing the park in the east will equalize the ratios—and putting it in the west would further skew them.

Let's modify the case by adding some more facts about the town. Although there are roughly as many easterners as westerners, the two communities are very different. The east bank is inhabited by affluent families. It also boasts a number of private clubs. Many of the families belong to one of them. The mean income on the west bank is significantly lower, and private facilities aren't found there. Westerners rely on the public parks.

Now, it seems, the mayor's decision should be different. The arithmetic she does, whether she is a utilitarian or some other kind of consequentialist, ought to focus on something else. The ratio of parks to people is no longer the appropriate number. What's needed is a measure of access to recreational facilities, one that factors in the possibility of going to a private club. It isn't easy to decide just what that measure should be. All sorts of considerations might come into play. The duty of the town to provide public facilities for all. The costs incurred by buying a private membership. The quality of the service provided when parks are overcrowded or distant. And more. Is there an obvious way to balance them? Or a unique, correct way?

The decision is no longer as easy. Nevertheless, the information is relevant. If our mayor had ignored it or didn't bother to inquire into differences between the two banks, she would have been derelict in pursuing the responsibilities of her office. *Objectively* right action, for the consequentialist, consists in choosing the outcome with the highest value. *Subjectively* right action is a matter of achieving the outcome *expected* to be best. Expectations, however, can be formed hastily or carefully. How they are formed matters to the moral status of the choice.

We can imagine a spectrum of mayors. For the slap-happy, the numbers in the two populations, east and west, are enough. Others probe more deeply. Some are exceptionally, even obsessively, concerned with smaller differences. Among them are people who discover the small, marginalized, desperately poor, minority enclave on the east bank, miles from the nearest park and with no public transportation to take children there. Taking that into account further complicates the arithmetic.

Is there a correct place to occupy on the thoroughness-of-research spectrum? How much work should the mayor and her council undertake before they make their decision? Of course, the more time they devote to this one issue, the less they'll be able to spend in resolving others. They seem to face a metalevel decision problem. How are they to budget their time? As devout consequentialists, they want to achieve the best available distribution of effort so that the individual decisions they take generate the optimal set of outcomes. Of course, to decide how much effort to put where, they ought to investigate, to find out the relative importance of the various issues. And they will have to decide how thoroughly to investigate to make a responsible decision about that question. So, they will face yet another decision problem . . .

In the end, of course, they'll rely on settled ideas about what counts as doing enough for due diligence. They will use prevalent rules of thumb, or "secondary principles," as Mill calls them, both in assessing how much attention an issue deserves and, maybe, how it should be resolved. *When*—and *how*—do the numbers count?

⸺⸺

As the eighteenth century drew to its close, Jeremy Bentham, the father of utilitarianism, introduced his ethical theory in reaction against the sentimentalist approach to morality then dominant in Britain. His commitment to reform was sparked, at least in part, by the recognizable social changes brought about by the nascent industrial revolution. Rural people who had hitherto supported themselves by spinning or weaving in their cottages (working in *literal* cottage industries) were undercut by the newly introduced machines. They flocked to cities to find, if they were "fortunate," jobs in factories—receiving starvation wages for long hours under oppressive conditions and living in the squalid accommodation hastily thrown together to house them. The contrast between their plight and the remarks of the moral sentimentalists, as they praised affability and conviviality and reported casually on the naturalness of warm feelings towards wealth and social grace, inspired him to want a more exact— and a more *widely* sympathetic—public morality. One in which "each would count for one and none for more than one." One that would replace sentimental indulgence for the privileged with a rigorous calculus capable of disciplining the "tender emotions." Bentham, I like to think, regarded David Hume, the prominent moral sentimentalist, as "eminently clubbable" in both senses of the phrase. Arithmetic was to be Bentham's club.

Mill, a prominent member of the club, provides a succinct account of the "Greatest Happiness Principle" on which utilitarianism is founded: "actions are right as they tend to promote happiness, wrong as they tend to produce the reverse of happiness." Let's concentrate on a difficult term in his formulation: "happiness."

With respect to happiness, Bentham was clear, straightforward, and blunt. Happiness consists in pleasure; the "reverse of happiness" consists in pain. Pleasure and pain are states of sentient beings. Human beings aren't the only animals who feel them. In the Western tradition, Bentham is one of the first strong champions of reforming the ways that people treat other types of animals. Indeed, if—as some of those who mourn the Anthropocene believe—human beings cause so much nonhuman suffering as to outweigh whatever pleasures our species collectively enjoys, Bentham would be committed to regarding our immediate extinction as a good thing. (Mill, however, although continuing to count the happiness of other animals, might well disagree.)

But how is the accounting to be done? Again, Bentham is clear—almost completely. When someone acts, the result is a state of the world, continuing indefinitely into the future. The relevant part of that long future consists in the time period throughout which some sentient beings are alive. You calculate the happiness generated by the action by considering all the states in which some sentient animal feels either pleasure or pain. Focus first on the states of pleasure. Each one will last through a time period and will have a particular intensity. Measure both. Multiply the two numbers to yield a product. Do this for each state of pleasure. Now add all the products. You now have the aggregate pleasure of the action. As with pleasure, states of pain have intensity and duration. Repeat the same series of measurements and calculations for all the states of pain. That yields the aggregate pain of the action. Subtract the aggregate pain from the aggregate pleasure. The result is the happiness of the action. If the happiness of the action is greater than that of any available alternative, it is the *objectively right* action in those circumstances. If it is at least as great as that of any other option, it is *objectively morally permissible*—an OK thing to do.

There—an algorithm. Not, of course, one anybody could ever deploy in advance to figure out how to act for the best. How would our mayor identify the vast distribution of pleasures and pains her choice will produce, let alone make all the measurements and do all the sums? Could she even recognize all the possible rival ways of proceeding? No matter. Bentham's standard isn't intended to guide action in every case. It is supposed to be the ultimate criterion against which our settled practices and habits—the "secondary principles" according to which we steer—are assessed. It is a touchstone that can sometimes be deployed in efforts at reform. Moreover, there are some instances in which people can fix a short time horizon for the principal results of their action and reasonably estimate that some particular consequence will dominate the calculation. As with the dynamics of projectiles, where physicists ignore the gravitational pull of distant objects and neglect wind resistance, a defensible idealization is sometimes at hand. Maybe that is true for the mayor as she mulls over where to put the new park.

Unfortunately, my reconstruction of Bentham's apparently simple theory retains one locus of imprecision. We know how to measure time. Intensity seems a trickier matter—many people find it hard to answer when doctors ask "where the pain belongs on a scale of one to ten." Let's be charitable. Suppose a scale has been constructed, and people know how to apply it. Now we must compute the happiness of a state. We'll multiply two numbers. But why *multiply*? There are many ways to combine two numbers.

Jeremy, James, and John are three utilitarians. They have measured the same two states. One lasted five seconds, at seven hedons (the unit for measuring both pleasure and pain). The other lasted seven seconds at five hedons. John computes the happiness by multiplying—as I just proposed. For Jeremy, however, if the period is x seconds and the intensity y hedons, the happiness is x^2y—for James, by contrast, it's xy^2. Jeremy thinks the second state is happier than the first, while James takes the first to be happier than the second. John believes them to be equal in happiness.

The various ways of doing the arithmetic stem from the two-dimensional character of Bentham's treatment of pleasure and pain. These states have both intensity and duration, and it is possible to give greater weight to one or to the other. For episodes whose values of length and intensity are both greater than one, Jeremy treats length as more important, while James emphasizes intensity. Each of them has innumerable utilitarian friends who share their judgment but who compute happiness by a different formula. The durationists and the intensivists come in many flavors and arrive at different rankings.

Even Bentham's simple version of utilitarianism can't offer an unambiguous standard for all cases.

Mill is clearly a consequentialist. He maintains that the assessment of actions as right or wrong is indissolubly wedded to the goodness or badness of the effects they bring about. Yet, contrary to popular as well as informed opinion, it is far from clear whether he is a utilitarian.

To be sure, his exposition of his views draws no clear distinction between consequentialism and utilitarianism. Perhaps he thinks of the consequences as measured on a scale of utility, so that Bentham's fundamental principle can be rewritten as identifying right actions with the maximization of utility, *however* utility is understood. If so, he is a utilitarian by fiat. The question remains: how far is his own treatment of utility from that of Bentham and other self-identified utilitarians?

Apparently, the difference is small. The principal departure of *Utilitarianism* seems to be the correction of Bentham's "vulgarest" flattening of pleasures. Mill tweaks Bentham by distinguishing the higher from the lower pleasures. He thereby adds another dimension to the enterprise of measuring happiness, introducing a further indefiniteness into efforts to apply the Greatest Happiness Principle. Now our calculus must not only decide how to weigh duration against intensity but also consider what extra weight the higher pleasures should receive. If the elevation of pleasures is measured on a third scale, three numbers will have to be combined to compute happiness.

Mill's short book *Utilitarianism* can be read as the exposition of a view inspired by Bentham. The task is to go beyond Bentham's crude conception of human nature, by recognizing the greater importance of the higher pleasures. In addition, Mill defends his departure from his predecessor and offers replies to the principal criticisms launched against the simpler (and inadequate) version of utilitarianism. Although it is less definite than that simpler version (because of the third dimension Mill has added), good judgment will allow people (people with fully developed faculties?) to fix the numbers and do the arithmetic (but, the mayor wonders, where does children's playing in the park belong on the scale of elevation of pleasures?). *Utilitarianism* provides Mill's moral views, and interpreters can use those views as the basis for exploring his social and political philosophy. Many of the best discussions of Mill's ideas proceed in just this way.

I pick up the stick at the other end. *Utilitarianism* is a work of defense, not of exposition. The position defended is consequentialism. In its most recent version, Bentham's, it has provoked many objections. One of those, the longstanding denunciation of assessing actions by focusing on simple pleasures, is correct. The critics are right to point out the vulgarity of that approach. Mill shows how to sidestep the criticism by making a simple amendment. After that, he reviews a number of faulty objections, offers a purported proof of the correctness of consequentialism, and shows how a consequentialist might understand the notion of rights. The ground has then been cleared for consequentialists to develop, insofar as they can, their preferred version of the approach. Mill's own favorite is not articulated in *Utilitarianism*. It has to be excavated from what he says elsewhere, when he is trying to advance views about how human lives should go and how societies should be improved.

"Absurd!" you might think. "Everybody knows Mill was a utilitarian—after all, *Utilitarianism* is the classic exposition of the position, routinely used to introduce people to it." The second point is plainly correct: the short book *is* a standard text. But why? I answer: because it is so obviously superior to its potential rivals. Bentham's *Introduction to the Principles of Morals and*

Legislation is quirky and long; Sidgwick's *Methods of Ethics* is ponderous and long. Mill, by contrast, is elegant, lucid, and short. Whether or not he was a utilitarian, he offers an excellent account of the tradition Bentham inaugurated. No problem in understanding why he wins the "classic text" award. So, perhaps, we should inquire whether here, as in other instances, what "everybody knows" is something *anybody* could *know*.

—

On Liberty is forthright in telling its readers how Mill will approach the value-laden questions that arise in political and social theory: "I regard utility as the ultimate appeal on all ethical questions; but it must be utility in the largest sense, grounded on the permanent interests of man as a progressive being." An obvious question: Why didn't Mill end the sentence differently? Why didn't he follow the semicolon with "I understand utility as happiness, but only when proper attention is given, not only to the vulgar pleasures, but also to those Higher satisfactions that distinguish human life"? Why drag in progress? Why fail to mention the connection between utility and happiness? Why the generalized attention to the human species?

Because, I suggest, "utility" has become a placeholder. It is a term used only to point to some scale on which options can be ranked. The "appeal to utility" is carried out by finding which available option achieves the highest value on that scale. "Utility," we might say, denotes whatever is to be maximized. Mill's sentence provides a little information about what that something is—we are to try to advance individual human lives and human societies as far as we can. A little information, but not very much. If, as I have complained, the tweaking of Bentham offered in

Utilitarianism introduces further indefiniteness, the sentence is even vaguer in suggesting how the consequentialist calculus is to be done. But, as we shall see, Mill has good reasons for gesturing toward an indistinct range of considerations—the features, whatever they are, that characterize human progress—and leaving the details to be worked out in the particular circumstances of decision.

Let's look, briefly, at how he articulates the "appeal to utility" in the subsequent chapters of *On Liberty*. The famous defense of free speech and open debate claims four good consequences: replacement of falsity with truth, extension of a partial truth to something more comprehensive, understanding of the grounds of an accepted truth, and full awareness of the significance of a truth. Presumably, these rank highly on the scale that measures "utility in the largest sense." But why? Because they bring people pleasure—"higher" pleasure? Surely talk of "pleasure" is out of place here. Not only because some truths are unpleasant, causing pain to those who accept them. Perhaps unfocused ignorance is always unpleasant—"I'm lost, all at sea." Focused ignorance is another matter. Some of the most exhilarating moments in the lives of investigators come when they feel they have finally posed the right question, that the path to further inquiry lies open before them. Moreover, many of the truths we come to know, important though they may be, are affectively neutral. At best, the alleged doctrine of *Utilitarianism* has to be stretched and strained to fit this "appeal to utility."

Or consider the passionate plea to cultivate individuality (the subject of chapter 3 of *On Liberty*). Central to Mill's argument is the emphasis on making your life genuinely your own, on the autonomous choice of a life plan, prepared by the full development of cognitive and emotional faculties. The extent to which the life trajectories of which Mill approves are full of pleasurable episodes or bereft of them is probably highly variable. The frequency of such episodes seems entirely irrelevant. What moves him is the thought of choosing (reflectively) the pattern of your life as one of your "permanent interests." A world in which those choices became more common would be an advance on the current state. A society fostering such choices would have made progress.

Or reflect on Mill's avowedly consequentialist defense of female emancipation. Relatively late in *The Subjection of Women*, he poses the question: What good would his proposals achieve? His first answer is hardly what might be expected from a card-carrying utilitarian: he points to "the advantage of having the most universal and pervading of all human relationships regulated by justice instead of injustice." Some pages later, having discussed other benefits—women's freedom, specifically their "free choice of their employments," use of a greater pool of human talent, the refinement of marriage, culminating in Mill's noble ideal of deep intimacy among equals—happiness finally enters the picture. That happiness is taken to derive from a psychological fact: when basic physical needs are satisfied, "freedom is the first and strongest want of human nature." From start to finish, Mill remains true to his conception of utility "in the largest sense," as *On Liberty* characterizes it.

In all three instances, the language Mill actually uses—"the permanent interests of man as a progressive being"—is apt, and its imprecision is remedied in the context of the topic under discussion. With respect to individuality, the interest in question is a fundamental freedom, whose character he is at pains to clarify. So too in specifying the good consequences of female emancipation. With respect to free speech, it is the value of truth. Believing the truth helps people navigate the world (a practical benefit), but Mill would surely not rest with that. He would likely endorse the eloquent response offered by T. H. Huxley to his friend, the novelist Charles Kingsley, who had attempted to comfort him after the death of Huxley's beloved firstborn son, with the promise of reunion in the hereafter. Huxley declared his resolve to "[sit] down before fact as a little child" no matter what "abysses" he might be led to. Whether or not truth yields exultation, Huxley and Mill view it as conferring exaltation. They see acquiring the capacity to face the truth as a form of human progress.

Throughout the entire range of his social and political theorizing, Mill's appeals to utility focus on human lives and the societies that shape them. *The Subjection of Women* rests on viewing the lives of women as going better when they have vastly expanded access to realms of public life from which they have been excluded. *Considerations on Representative Government* (for all its defects) is concerned with changes in social institutions to improve the quality of citizens' lives. So too, as we have seen, for the *Principles of Political Economy*. As Mae West might have remarked after reading Mill: "Happiness has very little to do with it."

For systematic reasons. The path from consequentialism to Benthamite utilitarianism has a large number of forks. At many of them, Mill's commitments lead him to take the road less traveled.

For consequentialists, the rightness or wrongness of an action turns on whether the action makes the world a surpassingly better place. More pedantically, an action is morally correct if it generates a world better than any other that could have been produced by acting differently. Benthamite utilitarians make the following assumptions about how you evaluate worlds.

1. Only attend to the future consequences of the action.
2. Only attend to the subjective experiences of individual beings.
3. Only attend to pleasures and pains.
4. Aggregate: the value of an individual's life is obtained by adding up the pleasures and subtracting the pains.
5. Aggregate again: the value of a world is the sum of the values of the lives of the sentient beings who inhabit it.

Mill can accept none of these.

The first assumption may appear to be a truism. "People can't change the past." Muddled fantasies about time travel to the contrary, that observation is correct. Human actions can, however, change the value of the past—and thus affect the total worth of the world. As the ancients already appreciated, the quality of a human life can be affected by events occurring after the person's death. Consider the tale of the prodigal son, as it features in many novels and films. A couple, devoted to their child, scrimp and save to foster the lad's development, allowing him to enjoy the education, the recreations, and the opportunities they never had. After their death, he falls into bad company, develops depraved habits, wastes all he has been given, and dies in painful penury. In light of the sad consequences, what had once seemed noble and generous acts of loving self-sacrifice are diminished by their sorry effects. They come to appear sad and futile.

Mill cannot accept the second assumption for several reasons. First, his conception of human progress recognizes the value of human social progress. In addition to the advances individuals make when their faculties are developed and when they choose the patterns of their own lives, there is a further good in the policies and actions that set in place social arrangements for fostering individuality. Second, besides the subjective experiences people have, the relations among them affect the value of their lives and thus of the world in which they live. The lesson Mill learned when he met Harriet Taylor is, as we have seen, reflected in his writings, in his concern with the emotions and with the "social part" of human nature. Third, the relation of subjective states to reality matters to Mill. Part of our interest as progressive beings consists in apprehending the truth, and a state of permanent illusion, however pleasurable, would be undercut by the failure to accord with the facts.

The latter points can be illustrated by a thought experiment. As the Christmas holidays approach, many groups of workers organize parties at which gifts are distributed. For any large workplace, having each person give a present to each coworker would be impossibly burdensome. Instead, everybody draws a name out of a hat and buys something for the designated person. Analogously, for any world with its distribution of pains and pleasures there are *Secret Santa counterparts*. In a Secret Santa counterpart, the same distribution of pleasures and pains obtains, but the causes of the pleasures and pains are randomly assigned. Perhaps in the ordinary world, you and I regularly give each other assistance. In a Secret Santa counterpart, each of us has the pleasurable experiences of receiving aid, but they come from a motley collection of sources. The relations among people are entirely disrupted. The bases of friendship—and of enmity—are absent. Important values, like gratitude and mutual affection, as well as their negative inversions, have vanished.

From the Benthamite perspective, nothing has changed. Exactly the same balance of pleasure over pain has been achieved. The Secret Santa counterpart is neither better nor worse than the original world. For Mill, however, that cannot be so. The lives of the world's inhabitants have been radically impoverished.

The Benthamite strikes back. "The description given is incoherent. You assumed the distribution of pleasures and pains to be preserved—but that can't be right. With the random assignment of causes and effects, people will not feel the same warm feelings toward one another—no joy in gratitude or warm glow from having aided a friend." Indeed, they couldn't have exactly the same pains and pleasures *if they had a correct view of what was occurring*. But they could if they were massively deluded. In the Secret Santa counterpart, the inhabitants will have the illusion of friendship and will feel gratitude where none is due. Because they are systematically deceived, however, the value of their feelings, and of their lives, is reduced, perhaps even to worthlessness.

Assumption 3 is problematic for reasons anyone who knows one of Mill's most famous sentences should appreciate. The oddity of counting the kinds of experiences Bentham overlooked as "higher *pleasures*" is masked when he focuses on poetry—it's easy to imagine Mill in rhapsody as he and Harriet Taylor read Wordsworth to each other. Elsewhere, however, his attempt to portray human dignity as "happiness" shows its strain: "It is better to be a human being dissatisfied than a pig dissatisfied; better to be Socrates dissatisfied than a fool satisfied." Better, perhaps, also for Freud to reject the drugs that would cloud his thinking and accept the pain of his terminal cancer as he continues to write. Mill's sentence surely reminds us that dignity and nobility and stoic perseverance are qualities enriching human lives, sometimes even the qualities that render those lives admirable. In some instances, perhaps many, they are all the more striking for the repudiation of pleasure and comfort that accompanies them. Viewing them as contributing to some "higher" type of happiness twists ordinary words. The price of Mill's efforts to stress the continuity of his views with Bentham's is a very bad pun.

Moreover, the characteristics distinguishing Socrates from the fool (or the pig) are not matters of episodes in Socrates's life. They are enduring conditions throughout long periods of his existence and sometimes of its whole adult extent. When someone is moved by a poem, we can recognize an event, in which something like pleasure occurs for an interval of time. If all the features Mill wanted to add to the Benthamite account could be reduced to this form, he could try to extend Bentham's arithmetic. Take the happiness to be a function of intensity and duration (which function?), and accommodate the "higher pleasures" by multiplying. Mill reads Wordsworth for half an hour, at an intensity of seven hedons. Bentham spends half an hour in the pub playing pushpin, also at an intensity of seven hedons. Because of the multiplier effect, Mill's experience makes for ten times the happiness of Bentham's. Socrates and Freud, however, can't be understood that way. Their dedication isn't linked to particular events but is a standing condition expressed for large parts of their mature lives. The same goes for John Stuart's love for Harriet. Moreover, the value of that love is magnified by its relations to features of his life before he met her (by the growth and flourishing stemming from that meeting) and after her death (by the times in Avignon with Helen, the daily visits to the cemetery, and Helen's loving editing of his *Chapters on Socialism*).

Once these points are appreciated, we can begin to see why Mill cannot accept either the fourth or fifth assumption. When he thinks about utility, he thinks first about what makes for human progress. That leads him to concentrate on human lives and on the societies in which people live. How do individual actions improve the quality of human lives? How do they improve the social conditions under which people develop and grow and within which they pursue their chosen "plans of life"? When he tackles these questions he doesn't decompose the life of a person or the trajectory of a society into small chunks whose worth can be aggregated to yield the value of the whole. Instead, he thinks holistically, considering the enduring features of lives, the relations among lives, the aspects of society that promote valuable lives. As book 2 of the *Principles* might lead us to expect, he is sometimes concerned with distribution.

Since the publication of *Utilitarianism*, Bentham's version has been refined by some of his successors. Instead of attending to transient states of pleasure and pain, they have sometimes considered other units—satisfaction of wants (or "preferences")—to which value can be ascribed, entered into the accounting books and totted up to deliver the numbers on which a Benthamite standard can base its judgments about goodness and badness, rightness and wrongness. The fundamental strategy of utilitarianism, in my view, is its commitment to aggregation. There's a calculus, and it proceeds by decomposition, valuation, and adding up. Mill breaks with that strategy. He refuses to take the value of a life as residing in some total sum of the values ascribed to a set of atoms, states that can be measured and assessed independently of one another. To have lived well isn't to have enjoyed enough pleasurable episodes, or to have satisfied enough of your preferences, or to have achieved enough goals, or even to have had enough days that have gone well. It is to have developed your faculties, to have chosen for yourself, to have constantly grown and refined your decisions, to have pursued your central aims with some (variable) level of success, and to have been someone with a unique mixture of the qualities that differentiate human lives from those of nonhuman animals. Including, significantly, interpersonal relations. Your contributions to the lives of others.

Mill is no utilitarian. He is a *flexible consequentialist*, someone for whom the numbers sometimes count, but in many different ways.

What exactly does this mean? How does it supply any touchstone for what individual people should do or how, working together, they should reform the societies in which they live? Let us return, once again, to the mayor and her musings about the new park.

Is it reasonable to suppose that placing the park in the west (say) would be superior just in case all the pleasurable or painful park-placement-experiences of putting it there add up to a greater value than the comparable total if the decision favored the east?

That's not a standard anyone could apply. Minds boggle at some determinate relation among definite numbers corresponding to the two aggregate values. Better to recognize the criterion as arising from factors a wise mayor could assess. She will give some weight, of course, to the fact that access to a park will issue in pleasurable experiences (also in some painful ones) both for the children who come to play and for their parents. The future episodes with the most significance, though, are those through which the children grow and through which their parents come to identify ways of helping their further growth. In the developing of physical skills. In increasing aptitudes for relating harmoniously to one another. In discovering talents and activities that will play an important role in a child's future.

So for this decision, our mayor takes what needs to be counted to be the degrees to which children have opportunities for certain types of growth. In exploring the question, she'll need facts about different subpopulations: the offspring of affluent parents who already have high degrees of the pertinent opportunities, the children whose families cannot afford the private clubs, and the young members of the marginalized minorities. She'll also need information about the likely effects of bringing different kinds of children together. Any picture of the situation she can compose will be revisable—she cannot pretend to certainty. Nevertheless, she can make progress by studying the composition of the various regions of the town and by consulting her local educators.

Many parts of what she needs to know would emerge if she had the opportunity to foster just that kind of deliberation progressive Mill sees as crucial to the harmonization of plans of life, to democracy, and to the assignment of resources. Indeed, if she could bring representatives of the potentially affected townspeople together, ensure representation of every perspective, equip the deliberators with any factual information they might need, and fill them with solidarity so they would attend carefully to one another's needs and aspirations, the resultant conversation would provide the best way to resolve the issue. Because she cannot do that, she tries to simulate an ideal discussion. The numbers she introduces elide differences she knows to be important but that she cannot measure. If she places the park in the west, so many children will be well served to such and such degrees. The arithmetic is done via estimates that override details.

Utilitarians typically follow the line of Mill's *Utilitarianism*. Exact numbers are unfathomable, and hence moral decisions must proceed by "secondary rules." The unknown (unknowable) arithmetic, however, provides the ultimate standard for the goodness or the badness of the outcome. Progressive Mill should invert that picture. Given his emphasis on autonomy, he should view the criterion for objective correctness as provided by ideal deliberations in which affected parties engage with one another. It is not something imposed externally but generated from within—a tribute to the autonomy he regards as a critical value. Because those discussions are impossible to arrange and hard to simulate with any close degree of approximation, decision makers must make rough estimates of how the factors they conceive as important *to the people who will be affected* add up and balance. In doing that, they sometimes resort to arithmetic. It looks as though amount x of increase in access to growth-providing activities will occur if the park is situated in the west and amount y if it is placed in the East—and the choice turns on whether x

is greater or less than *y*. (A tie should probably stimulate our mayor to investigate further and run the numbers again.)

---∞∞∞---

Utilitarians and other consequentialists are often challenged—"refuted"—by extreme cases in which the numbers appear to dictate a morally problematic decision. Caution is needed here. Cases beloved by some of Mill's successors, later moral philosophers, are remote—absurdly remote—from the conditions of human existence, and it is right to wonder if, under such bizarre conditions, our deliberative capacities are up to the task of generating reliable responses. A vast amount of ink has been spilled in debating whether an onlooker should flip a switch to divert a trolley so that it will not kill five people strapped to its current track but only the one person bound to a side branch. Or whether the same unfortunate observer should push a fat man from a bridge above the track to attain the same end. "Intuitions" about these stripped-down stories outrun whatever skills most people have to make moral judgments—if we try to think ourselves into the situations, it is entirely reasonable to feel uncomfortable (as many of the undergraduate victims of trolleyologists do). These are not the kinds of situations with which we have evolved, psychologically and socially, to deal. Our adaptive toolbox is inadequate to cope with them. And people who have not been steeped in an odd philosophical culture recognize the inadequacy. They squirm uncomfortably and do not venture a response, even when their professors put them on the spot.

Imagine yourself in the place of the observer. What would your immediate reaction be? Probably to try to signal to the trolley's driver. If you are certain that there is no driver, you would look around for something to block the trolley's path, an object capable of halting it or derailing it. You probably would not think of either a fat man or yourself as playing that role. If, by some quirk of fate you did, why would you think of the fat man as sufficiently heavy to succeed in it and yourself as too light? Why believe that shoving the fat man will land him in the right place? Why not plead with the fat man to join you in the jump? Standing beside the track, you might be moved to try to save as many lives as possible—and thus, in desperation, after failing to find any other remedy, flip the switch. But, standing on the bridge, you would keep trying to find material objects to serve as obstacles, thinking of that as the best thing to do.

Let's move on from the fantasies of trolleyology to more realistic examples, cases harder than the one facing the mayor, but with some articulable connection to the world in which we make our moral decisions. Sometimes, it appears, the only way to save a larger number of human lives is to sacrifice an innocent person. Here, we might think, the arithmetic is clear and definite. No need to ask what should be counted. The units for the calculation and comparison are crushingly obvious: human lives. Even Mill should acknowledge that. If the decision is to promote the quality of human lives in the ways he emphasizes, it is crucial to *preserve* the lives in question.

Consider, then, a group of surgeons, returning from a conference in some exotic place. Their plane crashes, but thirteen of them manage to survive and to reach a remote island. Fortunately, the island will support them indefinitely, allowing the prospect of awaiting rescue and eventually continuing their former lives. Sadly, however, twelve of the thirteen have sustained injuries to some important internal organ. Each of them can survive for several days, but, after that, each will need a transplant. By chance, the healthy thirteenth could supply all the organs required. Suppose they have managed to retain all the equipment necessary for performing any surgery, that the group of twelve contains specialists able to perform all the transplant operations, that they have resources to nurse the recipients through the postoperative period, and that they can work out a schedule for performing all the operations if the organs were on hand. (Such wallowing in fantastic assumptions is, all too often, a principal feature of philosophical thought experiments.) What should they do?

Utilitarians are accused of condoning a course of action many people find morally repellent. The twelve should kill the thirteenth, harvest the organs, and perform the operations according to the schedule. The numbers count. To permit twelve lives to continue is better than only allowing one of the group to survive. Assuming that he did not reject the scenario as overly farfetched, what would progressive Mill recommend?

That's not clear. Given his rejection of five major assumptions strict utilitarians make, his evaluation of the consequences doesn't simply count lives. We are to ask: would the imagined murder (committed as gently as you like) lead to a better world than the alternative in which, at various rates, the twelve succumb to organ failure? Since Mill takes into account the *ways* in which effects come about (recall the Secret Santa counterparts), he might view overriding the victim's autonomy as sufficiently awful to undercut the value of having twelve lives, rather than one, continue. Twelve blighted lives, the lives of murderers, don't weigh as heavily as casual calculators think.

Progressive Mill's ultimate standard for harmonizing conflicts works through deliberation. Among the very worst continuations of the story are those in which the twelve make their plans without giving the thirteenth any clue about what they have in mind. They pounce and kill and cut. Yet that is surely not the only option. Before they start sharpening their scalpels, they might talk. There must surely be enough time for discussion. After all, they have to acquire a significant amount of information about thirteen variously healthy and damaged bodies—and, contrary to philosophical fiction, the information doesn't simply descend from the air.

How does the conversation go? Perhaps through each of the thirteen explaining in turn why they want a continued life, with luck one that returns them to their former homes. As they listen to one another, different schemes for transplanting organs may come under consideration, a possible sequence of transplants that would by no means be risk-free but that might provide chances of survival for all. Suppose, however, that cannot be found. At the end of the day, it looks as though the only possibility for twelve to survive is to harvest all the organs the twelve need from the unlucky thirteenth.

The story could continue in a large number of ways. Having heard the details of the others' lives, the potential victim might consent to the envisaged use of her body. (She read *A Tale of Two Cities* in her youth and recalls Sydney Carton's closing lines.) The operation is to be respectful and reverent—if the twelve are ever rescued, the world will learn of her self-sacrifice. Or she might remain adamantly opposed to the planned operation. Her refusal might inspire one or more of the others to audition for the Carton role. None of them can supply all the needed organs, but each recognizes how personal sacrifice might enable a greater number to survive. The deliberation concludes with an imperfect remedy but, again, with a voluntary surrender of life.

Or all may insist on the priority of their own lives. Nobody can manage the degree of mutual engagement required to save some of the twelve. As that becomes apparent, as they all reflect on their deliberation and its unfortunate outcome, minds may change. At some point, perhaps, one of them exclaims, "If none of us is willing to give up life to save others, maybe we all deserve to die."

Progressive Mill views that ending as deeply sad—and even worse if it inspires the murder that deliberation promised to avoid.

Which outcome would his flexible consequentialism select as the best? One in which deliberation leads to final—utterly sincere—commitments on the part of all. Every one of the thirteen is willing to sacrifice to allow for the survival of others. They briefly contemplate settling the identity of the victim by drawing straws. But the thirteenth then interrupts, by requesting the privilege: "That's silly. I'm the only one who can save all of you."

The resulting world is better not simply because as many people as possible survive. Through their autonomous choices, exhibiting the development of their faculties, cognitive and emotive, they have shown themselves worthy citizens of Mill's progressive humanity.

Progressive Mill's ultimate standard for moral correctness is the procedural one we have seen in action in his approaches to freedom, democracy, and inequality. It involves qualitative judgments. At various stages of the procedure, numerical calculations, applied, depending on context, to many different kinds of things, may play a helpful role.

When and how do the numbers count? Sometimes, and in a variety of ways. They can never be the whole story.

Coda

Progressive Mill

William James was not only one of America's greatest thinkers; he was also an astute reader of other philosophers. His pioneering lectures, published as *Pragmatism*, begin with an insightful dedication: "To the Memory of John Stuart Mill from whom I first learned the pragmatic openness of mind and whom my fancy likes to picture as our leader were he alive today."

Progressive Mill, as I have portrayed him, corresponds to James's image—a figure whose work is directed toward the goals later pursued by the American pragmatists, James and John Dewey in particular. They, like him, have a deep concern with human progress and understand that progress in similar terms.

Many scholars who work on Mill may well feel that I have pushed him too far toward the pragmatists. I reply: the kinship is already present in Mill's own writings. I have not stuffed words into his mouth or thoughts into his head. The words are printed and the thoughts expressed upon his pages. They are especially prominent in chapters 1 and 3 of *On Liberty*, in the *Principles*, in *Subjection of Women*, even in the muddles and blunders of *Considerations on Representative Government*. They permeate the inaugural address he gave at St. Andrews. They occur in brief flashes in his essays on literature and the arts.

If those features are not usually emphasized by Mill's interpreters, that is because their own readings are differently selective. Holding that his approach to moral philosophy is given in *Utilitarianism* and that the departure from Bentham was relatively small, they use the resultant version of utilitarianism to reconstruct his approach to social and political questions. The remarks about "utility in the largest sense" and "highly developed faculties" are written off as rhetorical flourishes—window dressing for a clear and definite moral stance.

Nobody who thinks the twin essays on Bentham and Coleridge provide important clues to Mill's intellectual development should pursue that line of interpretation. Since I think they do, I don't. But this is not to launch a new campaign: progressive Mill as the Real Thing.

Half a century ago, when I was still a graduate student, the (then) doyen of British philosophy, P. F. Strawson, heard me present a paper on Kant's philosophy of mathematics. Strawson's book on Kant, *The Bounds of Sense*, had appeared in the previous decade, revolutionizing Kant scholarship, and I anticipated the challenges he would offer to my interpretation. He remained silent during the discussion but, at the end, came up to me and, to my surprise, invited me to lunch. I was even more astonished by the way he opened our lunchtime conversation. Instead of confronting me with objections (in the testosterone-charged fashion of the day), he began by musing on the agreements and divergences between "my Kant and your Kant," as he put it. It was a remarkably generous and constructive conversation, perhaps comparable to that an established director of Shakespeare might have with a younger colleague about "my *Lear* and your *Lear*."

No sensible director would ever claim to have produced the definitive version of *King Lear*, any more than a critic would pretend to offer the definitive reading of *Ulysses* or a pianist the definitive performance of a Beethoven sonata. For each of these works, there are innumerable misinterpretations but several, perhaps many, enlightening ones. Why should great philosophical texts be different? As I have grown older, Strawson's attitude has seemed ever wiser to me. There are many Kants—and, I suggest, several Mills.

Progressive Mill is one of them. Moreover, when we imagine him behind the impressive brow (framed by those odd tufts of hair), the man who peers out at us from the picture *does* have valuable things to say, not just to philosophers but to anyone concerned with the social, political, and moral challenges of our age.

Suggestions for Further Reading

Mill's writings have attracted an extensive body of appreciative critical discussion, and much of it is of high quality. Four books, in particular, stand out. John Skorupski's *Why Read Mill Today?* intends to show Mill's continued relevance to contemporary philosophy. I like to think that my chapters will parallel his, aimed for students and general readers rather than for professional philosophers. David Brink's *Mill's Progressive Principles* clearly recognizes Mill's role as a political progressive and develops an admirably clear and precise account of his philosophy as guided by this role. My version of progressive Mill differs from his primarily in viewing *On Liberty* as the key to understanding the notion of utility and in emphasizing the affective and social dimensions of Mill's conception of progress. Alan Ryan's *J. S. Mill* is a classic study, from which anyone concerned with Mill can learn much. Nicholas Capaldi's *John Stuart Mill: A Biography* not only supplies rich information about Mill's life but is also outstandingly comprehensive in recognizing the full range of his thought and in revealing the interconnections among his works.

The Cambridge Companions often offer excellent introductions to major thinkers from the past, and the volume on Mill, edited by John Skorupski, is one of the highlights of the series. It contains a number of articles that illuminate various aspects of Mill's thought.

For details of Mill's life, his *Autobiography* is an indispensable source. The correspondence with Harriet Taylor, edited by Friedrich Hayek, is also well worth consulting.

Index